(IN) JUSTICE
FOR JUVENILES

(IN) JUSTICE FOR JUVENILES

Rethinking the Best Interests of the Child

by

IRA M. SCHWARTZ
University of Michigan

Lexington Books

D.C. Heath and Company • Lexington, Massachusetts • Toronto

Library of Congress Cataloging-in-Publication Data

Schwartz, Ira M.
  (In)justice for juveniles: rethinking the best interests of the child / Ira M. Schwartz.
  p.   cm.
  Includes bibliographies and index.
  ISBN 0-669-14963-2 (alk. paper). ISBN 0-669-14964-0 (pbk. : alk. paper)
  1. Juvenile justice, Administration of—United States.   I. Title.
II. Title: Injustice for juveniles.
HV9104.S3286 1989
364.3'6'0973—dc19   88-15049
                                                                              CIP

Copyright © 1989 by Ira M. Schwartz

Published simultaneously in Canada
Printed in the United States of America
Casebound International Standard Book Number: 0-669-14963-2
Paperbound International Standard Book Number: 0-669-14964-0
Library of Congress Catalog Card Number: 88-15049

The paper used in this publication meets
the minimum requirements of American National Standard
for Information Sciences—Permanence of Paper
for Printed Library Materials, ANSI Z39.48-1984.

89 90 91 92 8 7 6 5 4 3 2

For David and Amy

Contents

Foreword

M OST of us place the well-being of our children at the top of our personal priority list. We love them and are willing to make significant sacrifices in their behalf. However, when it comes to public policy there is a world of difference between what we feel personally and what we insist upon from our governmental institutions. If left unattended, this disparity will threaten the ability of the American people to make intelligent decisions through our democratic institutions. It will also threaten our position as a leader in the free world, our ability to compete in a global economy, and our opportunity to enjoy a strong domestic economy during the twenty-first century.

Our society as a whole values education. Yet, one out of every four young people who enters the ninth grade will not graduate with his or her high school class. This problem is especially acute for minority youth, particularly black males, whose school dropout rates are approaching 60 to 70 percent in many jurisdictions.

Americans wisely have invested in reducing the incidence of poverty and in improving both the access to and the quality of health care for senior citizens. This has resulted in a significant improvement in the quality of life and longevity for this age-group. However, at the other end of the age spectrum, the indicators are that children are not faring nearly as well. Children now comprise the largest impoverished group in the country. More than 10 million children are not covered by any form of health insurance program. Unconscionable as it may sound, the rates of childhood immunization for such preventable diseases as polio, measles, and mumps are on the decline. Even more disturbing is that reports of child abuse and neglect are increasing at an alarming pace. There were an estimated 838,000 reports of child abuse and neglect in

1977. The number of such reports increased to a staggering 2.2 million in 1986.

(In)Justice for Juveniles: Rethinking the Best Interests of the Child provides a vivid reminder that nowhere is the disparity between our professed personal concern for children and the insensitive public policy that confronts them more evident than in the nation's juvenile justice system. Ira Schwartz, perhaps as no one else in the country would have been able to do, has provided us with a well-documented and extraordinary account of the politics of juvenile justice at the federal, state, and local levels. It is an account of how billions in increasingly scarce public resources are largely being misspent under the guise of combating juvenile crime and protecting the public. For example, and contrary to popular belief, a large majority of the children in the nation's juvenile courts and youth detention and correctional facilities are runaways, school truants, children who are beyond the control of their parents, and relatively nondangerous and nonviolent delinquent youth. Also, tens of thousands of children are confined each year in adult jails and police lockups. Many of these children are guilty of little more than running away from an intolerable and abusive home situation that often involves an alcoholic or sexually abusive family member. These very same problems were brought to the attention of the United States Senate Subcommittee to Investigate Juvenile Delinquency, which I was privileged to chair several years ago. Unfortunately, despite the efforts of some to change the system, in all too many instances today society responds to a child who has committed a relatively minor offense in a manner that increases the likelihood that a troubled child will become an even more troubled adult.

(In)Justice for Juveniles also draws attention to a new and particularly troublesome issue, an explosion in the numbers of troubled young people who are hospitalized for psychiatric and substance abuse treatment in private-sector hospitals. Professor Schwartz's research concludes that many, if not most, of the youth placed in these hospital programs could be treated more effectively and at considerably less cost with appropriate treatment regimes in the home and school or elsewhere in the community. Particularly troubling is that many of these programs are unmonitored and that some of the hospital programs are abusive and degrading, as well as ineffective.

Finally, this book does not leave the reader feeling totally hopeless. It contains a blueprint for action. It is a blueprint that is built on a solid foundation of research as well as the experiences in states all across the country. It is an agenda that elected public officials, juvenile justice professionals, child advocates, public interest groups, concerned parents and the public-at-large must attend to.

—Senator Birch Bayh

Preface

W HAT started out for me nearly 20 years ago as a career in
juvenile justice has gradually turned into a pursuit of justice
for children. Although the U.S. Supreme Court has declared that
children are entitled to some of the same due process and procedural
protections accorded to adults, the rights of young people are being
violated every day in many, if not most, jurisdictions throughout the
country. Despite class action lawsuits attacking the conditions under
which juveniles are confined, unprofessional and abusive practices
are commonplace in public and private youth detention and correctional facilities.

This book explores the recent political history of juvenile justice in
America. It examines the policies and trends in juvenile justice
during the pasts two decades and lays out a reform agenda for the
future, an agenda that I believe will bring us closer to the goal of
providing justice for juveniles.

Acknowledgments

D ozens of people from throughout the United States and abroad contributed in various ways to this book. To all of them, I give my heartfelt thanks.

There are a few whose contributions were so valuable that I would like to mention them specifically. Birch Bayh, former U.S. senator from Indiana and former chairman of the U.S. Senate Subcommittee to Investigate Juvenile Delinquency, provided me with important information regarding the history and development of the Juvenile Justice and Delinquency Prevention Act of 1974. Mark Davis, former congressional liaison for the Office of Juvenile Justice and Delinquency Prevention, and John Wilson, associate general counsel of the Department of Justice, furnished me with essential official publications and documents and shared their recollections about and personal experiences with the federal juvenile justice program.

Professors Gideon Fishman, Andrew Rutherford, Gary Melton, and Barry Feld reviewed selected chapters and gave me their candid reactions and suggestions. Professors C. Ronald Huff and Rosemary Sarri and Judge Frank Orlando reviewed the entire manuscript. Their comments and feedback proved especially helpful. Lee Eddison critiqued and helped edit the entire volume. Although these criticisms were sometimes difficult to take, they were invariably right, and I was forced to "go back to the drawing board" on more occasions than I would care to admit.

Laurie Levi, Linda Harris, and Moo-Sung Chung provided me with critical and careful research assistance, the kind of assistance one can expect only from first-rate graduate students. Danielle Hogston and Joel Thingvall provided expert and fast word processing, thoughtful editorial suggestions, and, most important, perspective and wit throughout the entire project.

I am also deeply indebted to Dirk Wales, a sensitive and compassionate man who helped me realize that I might have something worthwhile to say.

Finally, I must thank my family for putting up with me during the year and a half it took me to write this book. They were tolerant when I wasn't. They were understanding when I needed it. Without their support, I never would have finished the task.

1

While the Reformers Slept

I T is fashionable to say that Washington, D.C. is not the seat of all wisdom and knowledge. The problem is that too few presidents, senators, members of Congress, cabinet officers, presidential appointees, congressional staffers, and staff members of professional associations and public interest groups really believe it. Despite their periodic anti-Washington rhetoric, they see the federal government as the standard-bearer and themselves as the key players in the formulation and implementation of enlightened public policies.

Approximately fifteen years ago, President Gerald R. Ford signed into the law the Juvenile Justice and Delinquency Prevention Act of 1974. The act represented a major triumph for those concerned with the plight of children and those interested in reforming the juvenile justice system in the United States. To them, the act meant that the problems and issues confronting the juvenile justice system had finally been put on the national domestic public policy agenda and that the federal government would be expected to play a key leadership role in helping to bring about the needed changes.

The recent history of juvenile justice, particularly the period leading up to and following the enactment of the federal act, indicates that the national government is more a follower than a leader in the development of juvenile justice policy. More troubling, however, is the fact that the events that took place during this period also give reason to believe that the so-called juvenile justice system may in reality be something quite different from what its name implies.

Rude Awakening

I was sworn in as administrator of the Office of Juvenile Justice and Delinquency Prevention (OJJDP) on January 8, 1980. I was immediately confronted with the fact that the Juvenile Justice and Delinquency Prevention Act of 1974 was coming up for reauthorization. I wasn't too worried about it, because it was generally felt that the legislation had had a significant impact throughout the country. One of the major objectives of the act was to encourage states to prohibit the incarceration of status offenders (that is, runaways, habitual truants, and youth in conflict with their parents) and dependent and neglected youth in adult jails, juvenile detention centers and training schools. The indications were that tremendous progress had been achieved in this area. Moreover, the federal juvenile justice program enjoyed strong bipartisan support in the U.S. Senate and House and had the backing of juvenile justice professionals, public interest groups, national youth-serving organizations, civic groups, child advocates, and state juvenile justice advisory committees throughout the country.

In preparation for the reauthorization hearings, I convened a meeting of the top management staff in the office. I told them that I wanted to put some information together that would tell "the juvenile justice story." I told them that I wanted to inform the appropriate congressional oversight committees about the significant yield Congress had received for its modest investment in the program.[1]

I asked the staff to prepare a few charts that would show (1) how many youth had been admitted to adult jails, juvenile detention centers, and training schools in 1975, a year after the act was passed and how many of them were status offenders and dependent and neglected youth; (2) how many youth were admitted to jails, detention centers, and training schools in 1979 and how many of them were status offenders and dependent and neglected youth; and (3) how much money the office had given out between 1975 and 1979 and what the bottom line was.

The staff liked the idea and assured me that the data were available. I assigned Buddy Howell, director of the National Institute of Juvenile Justice and Delinquency Prevention—the research arm of the OJJDP—the task of putting the information together and asked him to let me know when the charts were ready. He called me a couple of weeks later, and I set up another meeting with the group.

Howell put the charts up on the walls in my office. After a few moments, I noticed that everyone in the room was staring down at the table rather than at the charts. Some were noticeably embarrassed. A few of the staff members looked around to see the reactions of the others.

I studied the charts carefully and was stunned by what I saw. I looked at Howell and said, "What the hell is this? You mean to tell me that after all the money the office has given out, and after a 75 percent reduction in admissions for status offenders, the overall rate of admissions in these places was about the same in 1979 as in 1975?" Howell replied, "Ah, well, yes, that's what the data suggest."

I, along with many others in the country who were connected with juvenile justice, had been under the impression that juveniles were being removed from institutions in record numbers. The charts showed otherwise. They were political dynamite.

I asked if the data meant that kids were being relabeled. In other words, were the juveniles who used to be labeled status offenders now being called delinquents? The staff members didn't know for sure; they speculated that some of this might be going on. I remember saying that it was my understanding that rates of serious juvenile crime in the United States had stabilized. I asked whether serious juvenile crime rates were increasing and if that accounted for the continued high rates of admissions. I was told that we weren't in the midst of a big juvenile crime wave.

Trying to get answers was like pulling teeth. It was obvious that no one wanted to talk about the data or what the figures meant. I adjourned the meeting and told Howell to take the charts with him and keep them in his office.

Here I was, freshly appointed to the top juvenile justice job in the country. One of my immediate priorities was to lead the charge to see that the Juvenile Justice and Delinquency Prevention Act of 1974 was reauthorized by Congress. No one expected this to be a particularly difficult task, since virtually everyone was claiming that the federal juvenile justice program was a success story. I now had serious doubts about just how successful the program really was. Unfortunately, some of my worst suspicions turned out to be true.

Great Expectations

In 1974, when Congress enacted the Juvenile Justice and Delinquency Prevention Act, the legislation passed by overwhelming majorities in both the House and the Senate, signaling that juvenile justice reform had become a national priority.[2] According to former U.S. senator Birch Bayh, the chief architect of the legislation, "the Act [recognized] that our present system of juvenile justice [was] failing miserably."[3] The legislation was "designed specifically to prevent young people from entering our failing juvenile justice system, and to assist communities in developing more sensible and economic approaches for youngsters already in the juvenile justice system."[4]

The act mandated that status offenders, dependent and neglected youth, and abused youth be removed from adult jails, detention centers, and training schools—that juveniles could not be housed in facilities where they would have regular contact with adult criminal offenders.[5] It required that the newly created Office of Juvenile Justice and Delinquency Prevention coordinate all federal delinquency prevention and control efforts and give leadership and support for research, provide training for juvenile justice professionals, and give technical assistance to state and local policymakers and practitioners. The act also encouraged the development of community-based alternatives to the institutionalization of nonviolent and nondangerous delinquent youth. Although participation in the federal juvenile delinquency program was voluntary on the part of the states, their receipt of federal funds was tied to the achievement of specific objectives.[6]

The enactment of the Juvenile Justice and Delinquency Prevention Act of 1974 gave reformers a tremendous boost. It put the weight of the federal government, coupled with the "carrot-and-stick" approach, behind desperately needed changes. The optimism the act generated was reflected in the comments of those calling for the reforms. For example, John M. Rector, administrator of the OJJDP during the first two years of the Carter administration, testified before Congress in 1978 that "something in the neighborhood of 90 percent of [the] youths . . . who were incarcerated, could be handled in community-based programs."[7] He said that he hoped to use the resources of the office to replicate the experience in Massachusetts and "persuade a few other states to deinstitutionalize statewide their large juvenile correction institutions."[8] Milton Rector (no relation to John M. Rector), then president of the prestigious National Council on Crime and Delinquency (NCCD), told Congress:

> In 1972, NCCD testified that the purpose and the goals of the Act were harmonious with the will of the American people. We believed citizens throughout this country were unaware of the abusive practices being condoned in the name of justice. We believed education on the status offender issue would stimulate an interested citizenry willing to monitor implementation and support community responsibility for these youths. We believed that community-based services would prove as effective as institutionalized settings and provide more humane treatment. Our beliefs were well-founded. There is little doubt that the will to deinstitutionalize youth is felt throughout our nation and will continue.[9]

Winds of Change

Although the Juvenile Justice and Delinquency Prevention Act was viewed as the major instrument for precipitating reforms, the winds of change had actually started to blow much earlier. Beginning with *Kent v. United States* in 1966 and *In re Gault* in 1967, the U.S. Supreme Court had issued a string of decisions that began "to define the constitutional rights of a class of citizens who previously were not believed to possess any."[10] For the first time, children had a right to be notified of the charges against them, a right to counsel, a right to cross-examine witnesses, a right to determination of guilt beyond a reasonable doubt, a right against self-incrimination, and a right to a hearing before they could be transferred to and tried in the adult courts.

Class-action lawsuits attacked conditions under which juveniles were confined. In 1970, *Pena v. New York State Department of Social Services* sought "relief for children subject to solitary confinement, to the binding or hand-cuffing of their hands and feet, and to the intramuscular use of thorazine or other tranquilizing drugs."[11] In 1972, in Indiana, *Nelson v. Heyne* challenged "supervised beatings, indiscriminate use of tranquilizing drugs without competent medical supervision, solitary confinement without procedural protections, mail censorship, and religious discrimination."[12]

In 1973, the federal court decided *Morales v. Turman* against the
Texas Youth Council:

> The court found that the defendant's practices of physical abuse, use
> of tear gas, solitary confinement without limitation, imposed silence,
> and "make work" details violated the Eighth Amendment prohibition
> against cruel and unusual punishment; that defendants' practices of
> mail censorship and use of English only violated the First Amendment
> freedom of expression provisions; that its transfers of juveniles to
> maximum-security institutions without procedural protections or
> hearings violated the Fourteenth Amendment due process guarantee;
> that racial segregation violated the Constitution; and that practices
> such as homosexual segregation, denial of contact with family and
> friends, withholding of case work, psychological, and other services
> from children in solitary confinement, lack of grievance procedures,
> less than twenty-four hour nurse availability, and poor personnel
> screening and training violated the constitutional right to treatment.[13]

The need for reform was also recognized by various presidential
commissions and national standards-setting bodies. In 1967, the
President's Commission on Law Enforcement and the Administration of Justice warned that both the increasing youth population and
arrests for serious youth crime were taxing state and local youth
corrections systems to their limits.[14] There were 220 state training
schools in 1965. They had a capacity of 42,423 and an average daily
population of 42,389.[15]

The commission predicted that there would be a 70 percent
increase in the number of youth confined in state and federal juvenile
corrections institutions by 1975. They reported that seventeen states
were in the process of building new training school facilities or
expanding existing facilities and that another twenty-one states had
such plans on the books.[16] The commission strongly encouraged the
development of community-based alternatives as a way of minimiz-
ing the potential growth in the numbers of incarcerated youth.[17]

In 1973, the National Advisory Commission on Criminal Justice
Standards and Goals issued its report. In an outright assault on the
use of training schools, the commission bluntly stated: "The failure
of major juvenile and youth institutions to reduce crime is
incontestable."[18] The commission felt that "the primary purpose to
be served in dealing with juveniles is their rehabilitation and

reintegration, a purpose that cannot be served satisfactorily by state institutions."[19]

The commission recommended that state and local policymakers and juvenile justice professionals follow the example of such states as Massachusetts and California. The commission noted that youth corrections officials in Massachusetts closed down that state's large juvenile training schools in 1972. They reported that several juvenile facilities in California had been closed as well and that officials "proposed that the rest should be phased out."[20]

Retrenchment in the States

While the federal agenda and the voices of reformers were calling for deinstitutionalization and the emptying of the training schools, an entirely different agenda was emerging in the states. Public outrage over the juvenile crime problem was generating tremendous pressures on state and local politicians, juvenile court judges, prosecutors, and others to take corrective action. The result was an avalanche of "get tough" policies and practices that were implemented throughout the mid and late 1970s and early 1980s.

For example, between 1978 and 1981, lawmakers in nearly half the states enacted legislation pertaining to the handling of serious and chronic juvenile law violators in the adult courts.[21]

> These statutory changes fall into three categories: (1) making it easier to prosecute juvenile offenders in adult courts (California and Florida), (2) lowering the age of judicial waiver (Tennessee, Kentucky, and South Carolina), and (3) excluding certain offenses from juvenile court jurisdiction (Illinois, Indiana, Oklahoma, and Louisiana). In addition, a number of states have attempted to stiffen juvenile court penalties for serious juvenile offenders through (1) mandating minimum terms of incarceration (Colorado, New York, and Idaho), or (2) enacting a comprehensive system of sentencing guidelines (Washington).[22]

The impact of these developments was both swift and dramatic. The rates of youth confined on any given day in juvenile detention centers (pretrial holding facilities) increased by more than 50 percent between 1977 and 1985. The rates for juveniles incarcerated in training schools on a given day increased by more than 16 percent during the same period.

The extraordinary increase in the incarceration rates in detention centers is the result of two significant developments. First, the average length of stay for juveniles confined on a predispositional status jumped from 9.2 days in 1977 to 11.7 days in 1984. Second, the practice of committing youth to serve time in detention centers, often as a condition of probation, has gained in popularity and is now used by juvenile court judges as a dispositional option in nearly half the states. As indicated in table 1–1, the rates of juveniles committed to detention centers skyrocketed between 1977 and 1982, when they appear to have leveled off.

Politicians, juvenile court judges, and juvenile probation workers justify this practice by claiming that committing youth to detention centers is a preferred alternative to committing them to training schools. It is also justified as a "credible response" on the part of the juvenile justice system and a means for holding youth "accountable" for their behavior.

The argument that the practice is an alternative to committing youth to training schools is dubious at best. Juveniles who are committed to detention centers are generally sent there for having committed minor and petty crimes; for probation, parole, and technical violations; and for disobeying a court order (for example, skipping school, curfew violations, running away, failing to obey parents, failing to cooperate with a probation officer). Juveniles who are committed to training schools are typically felony offenders. Because detention centers are high-security institutions, the result is

Table 1–1
JUVENILE COMMITMENTS TO DETENTION CENTERS, NUMBERS AND RATES, 1977–84

Year	No. of Commitments	Rate per 100,000[a]
1977	4,804	17
1979	13,323	46
1982	21,027	76
1984	18,977	71

Source: U.S. Census Bureau, Washington, D.C.: *Children in Custody.* 1977, 1979, 1982, and 1985

[a] Rate and calculations are based on the number of juveniles between age 10 and the upper age of original juvenile court jurisdiction in all fifty states and the District of Columbia.

that juveniles who are committed to these facilities are locked up under maximum security conditions for having committed relatively petty offenses or for having engaged in other forms of minor misbehavior.

The "get tough" measures that drove up the population of the detention centers and training schools had a particularly significant impact on the racial composition of these institutions. As can be seen in tables 1–2 and 1–3, there has been a substantial increase in the proportion of minority youth confined. In fact, minority youth now comprise approximately half of all juveniles confined in detention centers and training schools on any given day.

Little attention has been given to the impact of changes in state laws and policies aimed at making it easier to try juveniles in the adult courts. What is known tends to give a somewhat distorted picture by suggesting that the changes in laws have not necessarily resulted in stiffer sentences for juvenile law violators. In the only national study on this subject, researchers from the Academy for Contemporary Problems found that most of the juveniles waived to the adult courts had committed property and public order offenses. Relatively few (less than one-fourth) were waived for having committed serious violent crimes.[23] Moreover, their sentences were typically probation and/or fines, rather than jailing or imprisonment.[24]

New York State's Juvenile Offender Law went into effect in 1978. The law gave "adult courts initial jurisdiction over 13- to 15-year-olds arrested for murder, rape, robbery and arson. However, of the first

Table 1–2
DETENTION CENTERS: ONE-DAY COUNTS, BY RACE, 1977 AND 1985

Race	1977		1985	
	Number	*Percent*	*Number*	*Percent*
White non-Hispanic	5,573	57	6,975	50
Racial minorities and Hispanic	4,181	43	6,884	50
Totals	9,754	100.00	13,859	100.00

Source: U.S. Census Bureau, *Children in Custody.* Washington, D.C. 1977 and 1985.

Table 1–3
TRAINING SCHOOLS: ONE-DAY COUNTS, BY RACE,
1977 AND 1985

Race	1977		1985	
	Number	*Percent*	*Number*	*Percent*
White non-Hispanic	12,471	53	11,336	45
Racial minorities and Hispanic	10,937	47	13,722	55
Totals	23,408	100.00	25,058	100.00

Source: U.S. Census Bureau, *Children in Custody*. Washington, D.C. 1977 and 1985.

3,898 youths arrested for crimes subject to prosecution in adult court, fewer than 8 percent actually received adult sentences. The majority of cases were sent to juvenile court, or were dismissed on legal grounds."[25]

In a study of serious juvenile crime in California, Rand Corporation researchers found that "some jurisdictions such as Los Angeles clearly follow sentencing practices that make serious juvenile offenders as likely to be incarcerated as equally serious adults."[26] They noted:

> Public concern about specific heinous juvenile crimes has promoted proposals to permit younger offenders (14- and 15-year-olds) to be waived to criminal court. In most cases, waiving juveniles to the adult court results in CYA (California Youth Authority) placement, not prison. Consequently, reducing the age of permissible waiver could well create the aura of more punitive sanctions without producing the desired result.[27]

Although the stampede to change state laws to allow juveniles to be treated as harshly as adults has not had the desired effect in some jurisdictions, the impact in many states has been unmistakable. Juveniles have been propelled into adult prisons in record numbers. There were 1,445 persons under the age of 18 admitted to state prisons in 1981.[28] By 1982, the number had skyrocketed to an estimated 2,834.[29] Florida, a state where prosecutors have broad discretion in trying juveniles in adult courts, accounted for 769, or 28 percent, of these admissions. Staff members of the Bureau of

Justice Statistics estimate that the number of juveniles admitted to adult prisons in 1983 was between 3,800 and 4,000.

In a recent study of repeat and violent juvenile offenders transferred to the adult courts in twelve large urban jurisdictions, researchers from the American Institutes for Research found that "over seven out of ten of those convicted were sentenced to prison (63 percent) or the county jail (10.4 percent)." Also, those youth sentenced to prison received relatively stiff sentences, the average being 6.8 years.[30]

Returning to the "Good Old Days"

Another and more disturbing sign of retrenchment is the fact that many state and local youth detention and correctional systems are deteriorating because of neglect on the part of politicians and professionals alike. Politicians who have advocated "get tough" measures and have benefited politically from doing so have, in many instances, failed to appropriate the necessary funds to ensure that the incarcerated youth are treated and housed safely and humanely. Also, many youth correction professionals have proved to be extraordinarily weak-kneed and have failed to confront policymakers and advocate effectively for adherence to even the most minimally acceptable standards for the care and treatment of juvenile inmates. Facilities in many jurisdictions are overcrowded. Budgets, particularly for training schools, have not kept pace with inflation.[31] Monies for needed capital improvements have not been appropriated. The results have been a wholesale retreat from sound professional standards and practices, deteriorating physical plants, increased reports of abuse, scandals, and lawsuits.

In Oregon, before issuing his order, Federal District Court Judge James Burns visited the MacLaren School for Boys. He found:

> The cells were dirty and unsanitary. Students testified that the cells were infested with silverfish, cockroaches, flies and spiders, as well as body lice, and that the walls were covered with food, spit, blood, toilet paper and feces. The rooms smelled of urine.[32]

Solitary confinement was used excessively. It was being used for such things as " 'mouthing off' to staff, refusing to obey an order or directive, yelling or swearing, getting out of bed at night without permission—behavior, generally consisted typical for adolescents."[33] The court also found that "physical restraints, including handcuffs, leg irons and leather straps [were used] . . . unnecessarily and as a substitute for adequate programming and adequate psychiatric services."[34]

In New Jersey, Joseph DeJames, director of the Juvenile Detention and Monitoring Unit in the New Jersey Department of Corrections, met with members of the Mercer County Board on December 21, 1987, to discuss problems in the Mercer County Youth Detention Center. DeJames informed the board members that evaluation reports from his unit indicated that the facility was "characterized by violence, and a program whose mainstay of behavior management is the pervasive use of solitary confinement."[35] He pointed out that some alleged cases of child abuse at the detention center had not been referred to the appropriate authorities as required by law. Of the forty-three cases that had been referred to the New Jersey Division of Family and Youth Services in 1987, 50 percent were substantiated.[36] Also, DeJames and other critics of the detention center testified about the unusually high number of attempted suicides in the facility.[37]

Albert J. Hadeed, an attorney for Southern Legal Counsel, Inc., in Gainesville brought suit against Florida's training schools. Hadeed claims that he has seventeen pounds of abuse reports covering a twenty-six-month period. The suit alleged that staff members have "beaten or kicked children while they were shackled or hog-tied" and that children were left in "isolation cells lying on concrete beds, sometimes without sheets or mattresses, hogtied or shackled for extended periods of time."[38] The suit also alleged that "staff members encourage[d] larger children to assault or restrain smaller children as a means of disciplining and controlling them" and that tracking dogs were used "to hunt down children who attempt[ed] to escape from either Okeechobee or Dozier" and "dog handlers terrorize[d] and abuse[d] children" who were caught.[39]

In April 1986, it was reported that a 4-year-old boy was sexually assaulted by a 13-year-old in the Broward County Juvenile Detention Center in Fort Lauderdale, Florida. The young child was in detention because "his mother was hospitalized and could not care for him." The 13-year-old was in detention because he had been sexually abused and was awaiting placement in a shelter care facility.

Child welfare officials claim that a shortage of foster and shelter care resources forces them to put dependent, neglected, and abused children in detention. Some of those detained are babies.[40]

More recently, in the same detention center, a 14-year-old was sexually assaulted by his 13-year-old cellmate, who was being held on suspicion of murder. The assaulted boy, a burglary suspect, was ordered held at the center for twenty-four hours to undergo psychological testing. The youth's mother was informed that the center could not schedule the tests at that time and that the youth would have to be held in the center for a holiday weekend. The victim's mother said "her son was sleeping on a mattress in the cell at the center, plagued recently by problems caused by overcrowding."[41]

Steve Lerner recently examined conditions in California Youth Authority (CYA) institutions. His investigation led him to soberly conclude:

> The tragedy of the Youth Authority today is that a young man convicted of a crime cannot pay his debt to society safely. The hard truth is that CYA staff cannot protect its inmates from being beaten or intimidated by other prisoners.[42]

John Hurst, an investigative reporter for the Los Angeles Times, toured youth correction and detention facilities throughout California. In a shocking account, Hurst reported: "California's adult prisons, which confine some of the most dangerous convicts in the country, are, in some respects, more relaxed than juvenile facilities."[43] Even more incredible, he observed that adult inmates in California are not treated as cruelly as juveniles.

In San Francisco, a U.S. Department of Justice investigation concluded that the civil rights of juveniles were being violated in the San Francisco Juvenile Hall. Department of Justice investigators found inadequate supervision and an excessive use of solitary confinement, often for minor rule infractions. They found that youth were denied access to bathroom facilities, forcing them "to urinate and defecate on themselves or in their rooms." Also, youth were placed in "cold rooms"—rooms with inadequate heat—as punishment.[44] Several months after the investigation, a 17-year-old youth committed suicide in the facility. It was reported that the superintendent sent two juveniles, a 12-year-old and a 14-year-old, into the cell five days after the incident to clean up the mess.[45]

Recently, a suit was filed against the juvenile detention center in Orange County, California. The complaint indicates:

> Plaintiff Matt X is 15-years-old, and has never been adjudged guilty of anything more serious than malicious mischief. Since he was first interned at the Juvenile Hall on or about April 1985, Matt X has been assaulted, beaten, and tortured by the guards more times that he can remember.[46]

The suit alleges that "guards have frequently tied minors prone and spread-eagled on beds for as long as half a day as punishment." The youth are not even released to use the toilet. If the youth complain about being tied down, guards tighten "their bonds to cut blood circulation and to stretch their limbs, as on a medieval rack."[47] The suit also alleges that youth have been beaten by guards and that some youth have been placed in isolation for as long as three days without being fed.[48]

In Kentucky, Dominic Owens, age 14, was restrained by other youths for between twenty and twenty-five minutes during a "grouping" session at the Lincoln Village Treatment Center. His arms were crisscrossed under his chin and his hands were held above his head. Owens, who had a chronic asthmatic condition and an undetected heart ailment, stopped breathing. He was kept alive for eight days on a machine at a local hospital and subsequently died.[49]

A commission was formed to investigate the circumstances surrounding Owens's death as well as other alleged abuses. It unearthed the fact that incarcerated youth were being used as cheap labor. They were hired as tobacco hands on farms belonging to both state employees and private citizens.[50]

In 1985, U.S. District Court Judge Ray McNichols ruled that the disciplinary practices at the Youth Service Center (state reform school) in Idaho constituted cruel and unusual punishment.[51] Children were routinely handcuffed to metal bed frames, fences, pool tables and window bars by staff. They were "placed in isolation cells for up to two weeks."[52]

Also, youth were put in straightjackets and, on occasion, were hanged upside down from the ceiling by their ankles. They were often required to stand with their hands behind their back and their noses and toes against the wall from morning until evening, for days on end, for minor rule infractions.[53]

In the nation's capital, a lawsuit against the District of Columbia charged that "youths were beaten and subjected to unsafe conditions in the district's three juvenile institutions." A *Washington Post* investigation discovered

> . . . internal documents [that] showed that counselors at the city's Oak Hill maximum-security facility in Laurel routinely punished and improperly confined residents to their rooms for minor infractions. . . . Sharon Harrell, the city's chief investigator of staff abuses at Oak Hill, described Oak Hill as an "institution out of control" and complained that it was impossible to control its staff.[54]

In Oklahoma, orphaned and deprived children were housed in institutions with hard-core juvenile offenders. Juveniles were routinely subjected to verbal, physical, and sexual abuse. Hog-tying was commonplace.[55] The scandals in Oklahoma's juvenile training schools were of such magnitude that they precipitated two televised hearings before a congressional subcommittee. During one of the hearings, a girl testified that she had been made to remove her clothes in the presence of a male security guard and two female house parents. William Treanor, then a staff member for the subcommittee, testified that staff members in one of the juvenile institutions offered to let girls out in return for sex.[56]

In South Carolina, a recent report issued by the South Carolina Department of Youth Services indicates that the State's training schools are among the most overcrowded in the nation. Some of the institutions, particularly the ones that house youth with long commitments, had an average daily population of nearly 170 percent of capacity during the fiscal year 1986–87.[57] The report warned that "overcrowding, inadequate staffing, and the poor status of physical facility and living conditions pose the threat of a federal lawsuit."[58]

Discussion

There are some important lessons to be learned from the recent history of juvenile justice. One lesson is that federal juvenile justice policy lags behind developments in the states. Another is that the projections and recommendations of presidential or other national juvenile justice commissions and committees should be viewed cautiously, because there is a good chance that they may be out of touch with what's going on in the states. The 1960s and early 1970s were characterized by increasing youth populations and skyrocketing rates of serious juvenile crime. The 1967 President's Commission on Law Enforcement and the Administration of Justice sensed these trends and predicted that youth incarceration rates would rise accordingly. Just the opposite occurred. Training school bed capacities and average daily populations plummeted. Moreover, in 1972, while serious juvenile crime rates were still rising, Massachusetts got out of the training school business altogether.

In 1973, the National Advisory Commission on Criminal Justice Standards and Goals called for the closing of all large youth prisons and training school facilities. One year later, Congress enacted the landmark Juvenile Justice and Delinquency Prevention Act of 1974. Because it was estimated that more than 40 percent of all youth confined in adult jails, juvenile detention centers, youth prisons, and training schools were status offenders and, to a lesser extent, dependent and neglected children, the reformers expected that institutional populations would drop and that some states would follow Massachusetts' lead and close down their large juvenile correctional facilities. Again, just the opposite occurred. Public outrage over the juvenile crime problem precipitated an avalanche of "get tough" measures in the states. The rates of youth confined on any particular day in detention centers and training schools increased significantly. Also, the number of juveniles sentenced to state adult prison systems rose sharply. The movement to get status offenders out of institutions in the juvenile justice system merely resulted in removing girls from facilities, while the rates of incarceration for boys increased to take up the slack.

The current rhetoric out of Washington, D.C.—particularly from the Office of Juvenile Justice and Delinquency Prevention—emphasizes cracking down on juvenile law violators. Yet, as we shall see, in a growing number of states, particularly in the west and the south, policymakers and professionals are in the process of reexamining their juvenile crime control policies and moving to reduce their reliance on incarceration. This is yet another example of the disconnect between federal juvenile justice policy and the developments in the states.

The Juvenile Justice and Delinquency Prevention Act of 1974 has had little impact on reforming the juvenile justice system. This isn't too surprising, because it is becoming increasingly evident that the act was passed at the tail end of a major juvenile justice and, perhaps, broader social reform period. It was a period characterized by an increasing youth population and increasing rates of serious youth crime, on one hand, and advances in the area of legal rights for children and declining rates of juvenile incarceration, on the other. In short, the act was passed at about the same time that a large-scale juvenile justice deinstitutionalization movement was coming to an end.

The most important lesson is that the abuses and mistreatment of children that helped give rise to the child-saver movement at the turn of the century and subsequently led to the creation of the juvenile court continue to exist. The early child advocates and social reformers wanted children removed from adult jails and prisons.[59] They advocated for special institutions where children would be "protected" from the evils of society and exposed to proper education and discipline.[60]

They also advocated for a special court for children. They disliked having children tried in the adult criminal courts and being subjected to the rigors of formal adversarial proceedings. Instead, they envisioned a court that operated on a more informal basis and without the trappings of due process. It was also to be a court that relied on the work of probation workers and on the social and behavioral sciences to provide the information deemed necessary to properly diagnose and treat the causes of a child's delinquency or misbehavior.[61]

Unfortunately, the conditions in the new institutions for children turned out to be almost as oppressive as the conditions in the adult jails and prisons. Some of the juvenile facilities were architecturally modeled after adult penitentiaries. The daily routine typically consisted of strict regimentation, hard physical labor, and time for repentance. Laxity and disobedience resulted in severe punishment; children were often whipped, beaten, or placed in solitary confinement.[62]

Although the litany of abuses described earlier in this chapter is actually part of a long shameful history of mistreating children under the cloak of justice, the current situation in which we find ourselves is particularly ironic. It is ironic because some of the very same reform measures that were developed to alleviate the plight of children are among the most vocal and influential forces advocating for turning back the clock. For example, some juvenile court judges and youth probation workers are among the staunchest supporters of jailing for juveniles. They also support trying more juveniles in the adult criminal courts and increased use of adult criminal sanctions, even imprisonment.

Notes

1. The annual budget for the federal juvenile justice program was $100 million at the time I served as administrator. Approximately two-thirds of the funds were allocated to the states and U.S. territories that participated in the program, based on the size of their juvenile population. The remaining funds were to be allocated by the administrator on a discretionary basis for research, training, demonstration projects, technical assistance, and so forth.
2. U.S. Congress, Senate (1975), p. 1.
3. Ibid., p. 3.
4. Ibid., p. 2.
5. Ibid., p. xxii.
6. Ibid., pp. xxi–xxii.
7. U.S. Congress, Senate (1978), p. 55.
8. Ibid., p. 108.
9. U.S. Congress, House (1978), p. 460.
10. Bird, Conlin, and Frank (1984), p. 468.
11. Piersma et al. (1977), p. 612.
12. Ibid., pp. 614–15.
13. Ibid., pp. 617–18.
14. President's Commission (1967), p. 45.
15. Ibid., p. 143.
16. Ibid., pp. 38, 143.
17. Ibid., p. 38.
18. National Advisory Commission (1973a), p. 350.
19. Ibid., p. 358.
20. National Advisory Commission (1973b), p. 122.
21. U.S. Department of Justice (1982), p. 78.
22. Krisberg et al. (1986), p. 9.
23. U.S. Department of Justice (1982), p. 205.
24. Ibid., p. 208.
25. McDermott (1982), pp. 12–13.
26. Greenwood et al. (1983), p. 51.
27. Ibid., p. xiii.
28. U.S. Department of Justice (1984), p. 2.
29. U.S. Department of Justice (1985), p. 2.

30. Gragg (1986), p. 1.
31. Krisberg et al. (1986), p. 33.
32. *Gary V. Hegstrom* (1984), p. 23.
33. Ibid., p. 13.
34. Ibid., p. 27.
35. DeJames (1987).
36. Ibid., p. 1.
37. Ibid., p. 5.
38. *Bobby M v. Graham* (1983), p. 16.
39. Ibid., pp. 10, 12.
40. *Fort Lauderdale News* (1986).
41. *Fort Lauderdale News* (1987).
42. Lerner (1986), p. 12.
43. *Los Angeles Times* (1984).
44. *San Francisco Chronicle* (1986b).
45. *San Francisco Chronicle* (1986a).
46. *Matt X v. Orange County* (1986), pp. 4–5.
47. Ibid., p. 5.
48. Ibid., p. 9.
49. *Courier Journal* (1983a).
50. *Courier Journal* (1983b).
51. *Idaho Statesman* (1985).
52. *Idaho Statesman* (1983).
53. San Francisco Youth Law Center (1983).
54. *Washington Post* (1986).
55. Gannett (1982).
56. Ibid.
57. South Carolina Department of Youth Services (1987), p. 1.
58. Ibid., p. 2.
59. Schlossman (1977), p. 23.
60. Ibid., pp. 28–29.
61. Ibid., pp. 58–60.
62. Ibid., pp. 30–36.

References

Bird, J.R.; Conlin, M.L.; and Frank G., 1984. "Children in Trouble: The Juvenile Justice System." In *Legal Rights of Children*, ed. R.M. Horowitz and H.A. Davidson, pp. 461–514. Colorado Springs, Colo.: Shepard's.

Courier-Journal. 2 February 1983a. "State Alleges 'Unreasonable Restraint' Used at Center."

———. 8 April 1983b. "Delinquents Once Used as Cheap Labor, State Says."

DeJames, J. 21 December 1987. Statement to Mercer County Board of Chosen Freeholders Ad Hoc Committee to Study and Make Recommendations Concerning the Mercer County Youth Detention Center.

Fort Lauderdale News. 1 April 1986. "Police: Tot Abused While in State Care."
———. 26 May 1987. "Boy, 13, Charged in Jail Attack."
Gannett. 25 October 1982. "Oklahoma's Shame." Oklahoma City, Oklahoma: Channel 5. Film.
Gragg, F. 1986. *Juveniles in Adult Court: A Review of Transfers at the Habitual Serious and Violent Juvenile Offender Program Sites.* Washington, D.C.: American Institutes for Research.
Greenwood, P.W.; Lipson, A.J.; Abrahamse, A.; and Zimring, F. 1983. *Youth Crime and Juvenile Justice in California.* Santa Monica, Calif.: Rand Corporation.
Idaho Statesman. 12 June 1983. "Juvenile Shackled under Reform Rules."
———. 1 June 1985. "Cruel Punishment at YSC Finished, Federal Judge Says."
Krisberg, B.; Schwartz, I.M.; Litsky, P.; and Austin, J. 1986. "The Watershed of Juvenile Justice Reform." *Crime and Delinquency* 32 (1): 5–38.
Lerner, S. 1986. *Bodily Harm.* Bolinas, Calif.: Common Knowledge Press.
Los Angeles Times. 22 July 1984. "Unruly Youth Face Shackles, Isolation."
McDermott, M.J. 1982. *Facts about Violent Juvenile Crime.* Fort Lee, N.J.: National Council on Crime and Delinquency.
National Advisory Commission on Criminal Justice Standards and Goals. 1973a. *Corrections.* Washington, D.C.: U.S. Government Printing Office.
———. 1973b. *A National Strategy to Reduce Crime.* Washington, D.C.: U.S. Government Printing Office.
Piersma, P.; Ganousis, J.; Volenik, A.E.; Swanger, H.F.; and Connell, P. 1977. *Law and Tactics in Juvenile Cases.* Philadelphia: American Law Institute. Copyright 1977 by The American Law Institute. Excerpts reprinted with the permission of the American Law Institute—American Bar Association Committee on Continuing Professional Education.
President's Commission on Law Enforcement and Administration of Justice. 1967. *Task Force Report: Corrections.* Washington, D.C.: U.S. Government Printing Office.
San Francisco Chronicle. 24 February 1986a. "Horrid Aftermath to Youth's Suicide."
———. 3 September 1986b. "Justice Department Assails S.F. Juvenile Hall."
San Francisco Youth Law Center. 15 March 1983. Letter to Idaho Department of Health and Welfare.
Schlossman, S.L. 1977. *Love and the American Delinquent.* Chicago: The University of Chicago Press.
South Carolina Department of Youth Services. August 1987. "Report on Overcrowding: Juvenile Correctional Institutions."
U.S. Census Bureau. 1977, 1979, 1982, 1984. *Children in Custody.* Washington D.C.
U.S. Congress, House, Committee on Education and Labor, Subcommittee on Economic Opportunity. 1978. *Oversight Hearing on the Juvenile Justice and Delinquency Prevention Act.* 95th Cong., 2d sess.
U.S. Congress, Senate, Committee on the Judiciary, Subcommittee to Investigate Juvenile Delinquency. 1975. *Ford Administration Stifles Juvenile Justice Program.* 94th Cong., 1st sess.
———. 1978. Hearings on Serious Youth Crime. 95th Cong., 2d sess.

U.S. Department of Justice. 1982. *Major Issues in Juvenile Justice Information and Training*. Washington, D.C.: U.S. Government Printing Office.

U.S. Department of Justice, Bureau of Justice Statistics. 1984. *Prison Admissions and Releases, 1981*. A special report prepared by L.A. Greenfeld and S. Minor-Harper.

————. 1985. *Prison Admissions and Releases, 1982*. A special report prepared by S. Minor-Harper and L.A. Greenfeld.

Washington Post. 15 July 1986. "Settlement Set in Youth Facilities Suit."

Legal Cases

Bobby M v. Graham. 1983. Complaint No. TLA 83-7003, U.S. District Court, Northern District of Florida.

Gary v. Hegstrom. 1984. Unpublished Opinion for the District of Oregon, No. 77-10390BU.

Matt X v. Orange County. 1986. Class Action Complaint for Injunctive and Declaratory Relief, Central District of California, Case No. CV86-5693.

2

The Facts and Myths of Juvenile Crime

T HE juvenile crime problem shouldn't be taken lightly. Every year, thousands of innocent people are injured by young law violators. Some are killed. Hundreds of thousands of others suffer from having their homes or businesses broken into or from having their property stolen or damaged by juveniles. Moreover, the fear of juvenile crime has come to affect how we view young people, where we go and at what time of day, what businesses we patronize, and even our voting habits.

The juvenile crime problem is not simply going to disappear. The development of effective juvenile crime prevention and control policies will come about only as a result of informed debate on the issue by politicians, juvenile justice officials, public interest groups, and, most important, the public. At present, the gap between the public's perception and understanding of the problem and the reality of it is as wide as the Grand Canyon. This is primarily because what debate there is on this topic is characterized by rhetoric, demagoguery, and simplistic solutions. As a result, the public is often easily led and even stampeded into supporting policies and programs that are costly and ineffective.

Richard Daley, the politically ambitious Cook County, Illinois, state attorney and son of Chicago's late mayor Richard J. Daley, demonstrated what can happen when the public is not particularly well informed on this issue. In 1980, Daley announced that he was going to make the streets of Chicago safer by cracking down on the growing number of juveniles committing serious crimes. The result was that the number of juveniles committed to the Illinois Department of Corrections from Cook County increased by 119 percent in just one year.[1]

The John Howard Association, a respected criminal justice watchdog and prison reform group in Illinois, studied the juvenile crime problem and Daley's response to it. The association researchers did not find evidence of a serious juvenile crime wave in Cook County. Instead, they found that felony arrests for juveniles dropped 8.5 percent between 1975 and 1981. They found that fewer juveniles were arrested for murder in 1980 than in 1972.[2] The association also found that Daley's measures were particularly tough on the taxpayer because it cost nearly $11.5 million to house the additional juvenile inmates in the Illinois youth prisons.[3] The report concluded by saying that Daley's actions were "more a show of political expediency than responsible public policy."[4]

Politicians are not the only source of the public's confusion and lack of understanding on this issue. The public is also sometimes misled by the media—the very same media that are so diligent in searching out the facts and their implications in other areas (for example, catastrophic health care, the AIDS epidemic, arms control, the federal deficit, the Iran-Contra affair, education, tax reform).

Perpetuating the Myths

It was 10:30 P.M. on February 26, 1981. I was watching television and doing some paperwork when ABC's "Nightline" came on. Ted Koppel announced that the night's broadcast was about "crimes against the elderly." Being in the crime business, I put my work down and watched the program. I thought that the program was pretty good until a group of senior citizens from south Florida complained about all those kids who were victimizing them.

I wrote Koppel a letter in which I said that I enjoyed "Nightline" and found the program interesting and informative. I also told him that I was disturbed about the program I had seen because, contrary to belief, the characterizations regarding juveniles were inaccurate. I mentioned that the best available evidence suggests that juveniles do not commit a disproportionate amount of serious crime against senior citizens. I enclosed some material and suggested that he clarify this misunderstanding at some future time. I never received a response from Koppel. To the best of my knowledge, the inaccuracies have never been cleared up. The result was that millions of Americans were left with the impression that juveniles account for the bulk of the serious crime committed against older people.

Ted Koppel is a respected journalist. Although he can't control what people may say on a live television broadcast, it seems to me that he should have had a better grasp on the facts. And although the media must share some of the blame for furthering the myths about juvenile crime, the problem becomes almost insurmountable when government officials put out false and misleading information. Government statistics, whether inaccurate or not, are almost automatically considered credible in most quarters and are widely quoted.

Alfred S. Regnery, administrator of the Office of Juvenile Justice and Delinquency Prevention during the Reagan administration, wrote an article entitled "Getting Away with Murder: Why the Juvenile Justice System Needs an Overhaul," which appeared in the fall 1985 issue of *Policy Review*. In the article, Regnery stated: "About 30 percent of all people arrested for serious crimes are juveniles—a total of some 1.5 million arrests per year." He also maintained that juveniles—persons under the age of 18—commit about 2,000 murders each year.[5]

The facts are that persons under 18 years of age accounted for 592,372 arrests for Part I index or felony crimes (for example, murder, rape, robbery, aggravated assault, auto theft, larceny, burglary, and arson) in 1984. During that year, they committed 1,130 acts of murder and nonnegligent manslaughter, or about 8 percent of all such crimes.[6]

Regnery overstated the number of juvenile arrests for serious crimes (murder and nonnegligent manslaughter, forcible rape, robbery, aggravated assault, burglary, larceny/theft, motor vehicle theft, and arson) by more than 150 percent. He overstated the number of murders by nearly 75 percent.

Reprints of the article were distributed at government expense to elected public officials, juvenile and criminal justice professionals, public interest groups, and other interested parties throughout the country. In a "Dear Colleague" letter that accompanied the reprint, Regnery wrote: "Since being named by President Reagan to head the Justice Department's Office of Juvenile Justice and Delinquency

Prevention, I have tried to call attention to the system's shortcomings and have tried to suggest improvements." He hoped the article would "be helpful to those concerned about juvenile crime, those concerned with the juvenile justice system's ability to deal with such crime, and those concerned with possible solutions."[7]

To my mind, Regnery's article did neither. Instead, it misled people and increased the gap between the public's perception of the problem and reality.

Popular Myths

Although it is unrealistic to expect everyone to become an expert on juvenile crime, there are a number of common myths that need to be dispelled before responsible public policy can be developed in this area. Some of these are listed below.

Myth 1: The Rate of Serious Juvenile Crime Is Skyrocketing

In 1982, the Center for the Study of Youth Policy at the University of Minnesota's Humphrey Institute of Public Affairs commissioned a national public opinion survey on public attitudes toward juvenile crime. The survey, conducted by the Opinion Research Corporation of America, revealed that 87 percent of adults living in the continental United States believed that the country was in the midst of a serious juvenile crime wave.[8]

The best available evidence indicates that the rates of serious juvenile crime rose significantly during the late 1960s and early 1970s. The rates stabilized during the mid- to late 1970s, declined between 1979 and 1984, and increased for the first time in six years in 1985.

The rates of serious juvenile crime are high and should not be trivialized. However, we are not in the midst of a juvenile crime wave. Moreover, although the rates increased in 1985, it is too early to tell whether this marks a watershed and a reversal in the trends. Policymakers, professionals, academics, public interest groups, and child advocates need to keep a sharp eye on the rates of serious juvenile crime in the coming years and carefully consider their meaning and implications.

Myth 2: Juveniles Account for the Bulk of the Serious Crime Committed in the United States

The proportion of serious crime accounted for by juveniles declined significantly between 1975 and 1981. As table 2–1 shows, juveniles accounted for more than 40 percent of the arrests for serious crimes in the mid-1970s, and they accounted for approximately 30 percent of all serious crimes in the early to mid 1980s.

Myth 3: The Elderly Are More Likely to Be Victimized by Juveniles Than by Adults

Whether one looks at crimes committed by individuals or by groups, the elderly are more likely to be the victims of violent crimes committed by persons 21 years of age and over than by teenagers. Less than 30 percent of the crimes against the elderly by a single perpetrator are committed by persons 20 years of age or younger.[9] In crimes against the elderly in which there are multiple offenders, fewer than 40 percent are committed by persons under 21.[10] Also,

Table 2–1
ARRESTS FOR PART I CRIMES, JUVENILES AND ADULTS, 1975–85

Year	Arrests, All Ages	Arrests, Juveniles	Percentage Juvenile Arrests
1975	1,901,811	791,791	41.6
1976	1,787,106	755,650	42.3
1977	1,986,043	734,796	37.0
1978	2,169,262	778,166	35.9
1979	2,163,302	753,428	34.8
1980	2,198,077	684,143	31.1
1981	2,293,754	668,087	29.1
1982	2,152,480	625,514	29.1
1983	2,151,120	591,969	27.5
1984	1,834,348	570,648	31.1
1985	2,124,671	616,752	29.0

Source: U.S. Department of Justice, Federal Bureau of Investigation. *Uniform Crime Reports.* Washington, D.C.: U.S. Government Printing Office, 1985.

Note: The percentage of juvenile arrests may be slightly inflated, because the number of juvenile arrests includes data from police agencies that reported their arrests for one or more months (out of twelve). The number of arrests for all ages includes data from agencies that reported six or more months of arrests, which excludes arrest figures from those agencies without complete reporting.

what evidence there is suggests that "victimizations committed against the elderly . . . [are less] . . . serious when juvenile offenders [are] involved."[11]

Myth 4: The Serious Crime Rate for Girls Is Rapidly Increasing

The serious juvenile crime rates for girls increased significantly in the early 1970s, stabilized in the mid-1970s, and declined between 1978 and 1984. Like the rates for boys, they turned upward in 1985.

Myth 5: Juveniles Are More Likely to Attack Strangers Than People They Know

Teenagers are more likely to commit crimes of violence against other teenagers. Nearly two-thirds of the violent crimes committed by 12- to 17-year-olds involve victims under age 18.[12] In addition, teenagers are more likely to know or to have had some prior relationship with their teenage victims.[13] In other words, juveniles do not generally assault people at random.

Myth 6: Violent Crimes Committed by Juveniles Are More Serious Than Those Committed by Adults

The best available evidence indicates that "juvenile violence is considerably less serious in the aggregate than violence by adults. Juveniles use fewer weapons and less deadly weapons in their crimes and inflict less injury and financial loss on their victims."[14]

Myth 7: Minority Youth Account for the Bulk of Serious Juvenile Crime

Minority youth do account for a substantially disproportionate number of arrests for serious juvenile crime. However, arrest statistics are only an indication of the number of people who are apprehended by police. They do not shed light on the number of crimes committed that may go undetected or unreported or that may not result in an arrest.

One of the best sources of data on delinquent behavior is the National Youth Survey, a self-report study designed, in part, to get at the extent and nature of crimes committed by young people that may not come to the attention of official authorities or result in an arrest.

Data from the National Youth Survey indicate that minority youth, particularly black youth, do not account for a substantially disproportionate amount of serious juvenile crime.[15] However, minority youth who commit crimes are at significantly greater risk of being arrested and charged with a Part I offense than are white youth who commit similar crimes.[16]

Myth 8: States with Low Rates of Juvenile Crime Are States with High Rates of Juvenile Incarceration

Many elected public officials and juvenile justice professionals believe that high rates of juvenile incarceration correspond to low rates of serious juvenile crime. They feel that high rates of juvenile incarceration have a significant impact on general deterrence. Judge Peter Albrecht, one of the two juvenile court judges in Hennepin County (Minneapolis), Minnesota, recently surmised that the reason the juvenile crime rate is low in Minneapolis is that the county has a high rate of juvenile incarceration. Albrecht, in defending the county's policy of committing first-time burglars to a local youth training school, stated that the policy is designed to "nip [the problem] in the bud and give a fairly swift, relatively serious consequence on a first burglary."[17]

The existing evidence suggests that there is little or no relationship between the rates of serious juvenile crime and the rates of youth incarceration.[18] States with high rates of serious juvenile crime may have high or low rates of institutionalization. Conversely, states with low rates of serious juvenile crime may have high or low rates of incarceration.

Juvenile Crime Trends

The FBI Uniform Crime Reports are the most widely used measure of serious crime in the United States. The FBI statistics are a compilation of annual arrest figures submitted by state and local law enforcement agencies throughout the country for the eight Part I index offenses.

These FBI statistics are the best available national crime data. They are a good indicator of general arrest trends over time. However, as many who have examined these data know, FBI statistics have a number of significant shortcomings. Some law enforcement agencies fail to report their data to the FBI. Some submit data, but not for an entire year. For example, although 9,789 state and local law enforcement agencies submitted arrest statistics to the FBI for all twelve months in 1984, these 9,789 agencies covered slightly less than 180 million of the estimated 235 million people living in the United States.[19] In other words, arrests made in police jurisdictions that include approximately 55 million people living in the United States were not included in the FBI's published statistics for 1984 because they did not conform to the FBI's reporting requirements.

Also, published FBI statistics reflect arrests for crimes committed by persons under the age of 18. Although 18 is the age of majority, it is not the upper age of juvenile court jurisdiction in all states. The upper age of juvenile court jurisdiction extends through age 15 in Connecticut, New York, and North Carolina; through 16 in Georgia, Illinois, Louisiana, Massachusetts, Michigan, Missouri, South Carolina, and Texas; and through 18 in Wyoming. This means that 16- and 17-year-olds arrested for felonies in Connecticut, New York, and North Carolina are considered to be and are treated as adults. The same is true for 17-year-olds in Georgia, Illinois, Louisiana, Massachusetts, Michigan, Missouri, South Carolina, and Texas. However, 18-year-olds who commit felonies in Wyoming are treated as juveniles.

Also, it is important to keep in mind that juvenile arrest statistics do not reflect the actual volume of serious crime committed by young people. Juveniles "often commit crime in groups [and] the resolution of a single crime may lead to several arrests."[20] Paul Strasberg notes that this is particularly the case with respect to robbery. Strasberg's recent penetrating analysis of violent juvenile crime trends argues that "since robbery is the most common juvenile crime of violence, and also the crime in which group offending occurs most frequently, robbery arrests contribute most to an exaggerated perception of the amount of crime being committed by juveniles."[21] For example, there were 27,795 juvenile arrests for robbery in 1984.[22] However, fewer than 15,000 robberies by juveniles were cleared by the police during that year.[23] A more serious problem is the fact that arrest statistics do not account for the amount of "hidden delinquency"—juvenile crime that goes undetected or unreported or, if reported, does not result in an arrest.

Keeping in mind the limitations and difficulties in analyzing juvenile arrest data, what follows is an analysis of reported arrests for serious crimes by young people from age 10 through the upper age of juvenile court jurisdiction in all fifty states and the District of Columbia by the Center for the Study of Youth Policy at the University of Michigan School of Social Work. As table 2–2 indicates, the Part I arrest rates for juveniles were relatively stable between 1975 and 1979 and then declined until 1985, the first year the rates increased in more than half a decade.

These data are consistent with the findings of others. Delbert Elliott and his colleagues at the University of Colorado report that the findings from their National Youth Survey "clearly indicate that fewer teenagers of both sexes [were] engaging in delinquency in 1980 than in 1976."[24]

Table 2–2

JUVENILE ARRESTS FOR PART I CRIMES, NUMBERS AND RATES, 1975–85

Year	No. of Arrests	Rate per 100,000[a]
1975	791,791	2,695
1976	755,650	2,586
1977	734,796	2,528
1978	778,166	2,692
1979	753,428	2,620
1980	684,143	2,410
1981	668,087	2,399
1982	625,514	2,277
1983	591,969	2,182
1984	570,648	2,141
1985	616,752	2,356

Source: U.S. Department of Justice, Federal Bureau of Investivation, *Uniform Crime Report*. Washington DC: U.S. Government Printing Office, 1975-1985.

[a] Rate calculations are based on the number of juveniles between age 10 and the upper age of juvenile court jurisdiction in all fifty states and the District of Columbia.

The arrest data also indicate that serious juvenile crime is essentially a male phenomenon. As shown in table 2–3, the rate of arrests for Part I violent and property crimes has been consistently and substantially higher for males than for females. Again, these findings are similar to those of the National Youth Survey, which indicate "that males are disproportionately involved in delinquent behavior. This is true whether we use prevalence rates, general incidence rates, or offender incidence rates."[25] What is particularly interesting is that the increase in the numbers and rates of serious juvenile crimes in 1985 reflects increases in the numbers and rates of serious violent and property offenses for both males and females. Although it is too early to tell whether this uptick in the rates in 1985 is the beginning of a trend, it is something that needs to be watched very carefully in the future.

There are also a number of studies indicating that a relatively small percentage of juvenile offenders account for a disproportionate amount of serious juvenile crime. Marvin Wolfgang and his colleagues at the University of Pennsylvania have been conducting

Table 2–3

JUVENILE ARRESTS FOR PART I CRIMES, NUMBERS AND RATES, BY SEX, 1975–85

| | Part I Violent Crime Arrests | | | | Part I Property Crime Arrests | | | |
| | Male | | Female | | Male | | Female | |
Year	Number	Rate per 100,000	Number	Rate per 100,000	Number	Rate per 100,000	Number	Rate per 100,000
1975	69,682	454	8,641	61	576,452	3795	137,016	966
1976	63,270	419	8,112	57	550,959	3647	133,309	944
1977	61,027	406	7,429	53	535,158	3561	131,182	934
1978	68,626	459	8,042	58	563,091	4033	138,407	991
1979	66,893	450	7,957	57	548,760	3692	129,818	935
1980	64,101	437	7,863	57	495,824	3379	116,355	849
1981	63,956	444	8,057	60	481,354	3343	114,702	853
1982	58,651	411	7,565	57	448,667	3144	110,631	830
1983	56,020	399	7,121	54	421,292	3004	107,486	820
1984	53,510	388	7,143	55	403,137	2925	106,858	830
1985	58,225	430	7,322	58	435,565	3218	115,640	915

Source: U.S. Department of Justice, Federal Bureau of Investigation, *Uniform Crime Reports.* Washington, D.C.: U.S. Government Printing Office, 1985.

longitudinal studies in juvenile delinquency for more than a quarter of a century. Their findings, which have greatly enhanced our understanding of the serious juvenile crime problem, underscore the fact that a few offenders are persistent repeaters. Wolfgang and his associates followed two large cohorts of children born in Philadelphia in 1945 and in 1958. The first cohort consisted of 9,975 boys. The second consisted of 13,160 boys and 14,000 girls.

They found that approximately one-third of the males in each of the cohorts were arrested for a crime before their eighteenth birthday. Of those arrested, a substantial proportion turned out to be only one-time offenders. However, a small proportion (6 percent in the first cohort and 7.5 percent in the second cohort) turned out to be chronic offenders.[26] These chronic offenders accounted for a substantially disproportionate number of the serious crimes committed by each of the groups.

Other researchers have also found that only a relatively small number of juveniles end up being chronic offenders. Donna Hamparian and her colleagues followed a cohort of 1,222 youth who had been arrested for at least one violent crime in Columbus, Ohio, between 1956 and 1960.[27] Although this study focused on a very specific population, the researchers found that approximately one-third of the cohort were chronic offenders by the time they reached their eighteenth birthday. Moreover, less than 13 percent of the youth accounted for approximately half of all juvenile arrests for the entire group.[28]

Discussion

The juvenile crime problem is an issue that has managed to escape close public scrutiny. What debate there is on the topic tends to be dominated by rhetoric, a remarkable absence of hard facts, and politicians advocating for the "quick fix" or whatever happens to be the most politically expedient. Consequently, a large proportion of the billions in tax dollars that go into subsidizing the juvenile justice bureaucracy (for example, law enforcement, prosecutors, public defenders, juvenile courts, detention centers, probation and parole services, training schools, halfway houses, group homes, residential treatment centers) is wasted.

The greatest challenge to developing sound juvenile crime prevention and control policies lies in the development of an informed citizenry. Public interest groups, civic organizations, child advocacy groups, criminal and juvenile justice watchdog agencies, and interested professional associations need to launch aggressive campaigns to get the juvenile crime issue on the public agenda at the state and local levels. They need to educate and mobilize citizens to pressure policymakers to take an honest and objective look at the juvenile crime problem, to carefully examine how juvenile justice system resources are being allocated and whether they are being allocated wisely.

There are signs that this process is already beginning to take place in some jurisdictions. Policymakers in a few states and counties, particularly those faced with serious financial difficulties, are starting to turn their attention to the juvenile justice establishment. They are becoming more aware of jurisdictions with enlightened and cost-effective approaches, and they are starting to ask some tough questions. As more and more jurisdictions are confronted with limited resources and increasing demands for services, we can expect to see this process continuing to unfold in the years ahead.

Some criminologists and students of juvenile delinquency are predicting that the rates of serious juvenile crime will continue to decline or remain stable in the years ahead.[29] Their predictions are based, in part, on the fact that the at-risk youth population—children between the ages of 10 and 17—is shrinking. Now it appears that the pundits and "experts" may be wrong. The rates of serious juvenile crime increased sharply in 1985. Policymakers and professionals need to keep a close eye on this potentially alarming development, because it could mark the beginning of a new and disturbing trend.

Notes

1. John Howard Association (1982), p. 3.
2. Ibid., p. 6.
3. Ibid., p. 9.
4. Ibid., p. 3.
5. Regnery (1985), p. 1.
6. These data are derived from the *Sourcebook of Criminal Justice Statistics* (U.S. Department of Justice, Bureau of Justice Statistics, 1985) and from the Chicago

Police Department. Felony arrests for persons under the age of 18 in the city of Chicago were not included in published FBI statistics for 1984.

7. Regnery (1985), p. i.
8. Opinion Research Corporation (1982).
9. U.S. Department of Justice, Bureau of Justice Statistics (1986), p. 49.
10. Ibid., p. 54.
11. Hindelang and McDermott (1981), p. 2.
12. Ibid., p. 61.
13. Ibid., p. 87.
14. Strasberg (1984), p. 26.
15. Huizinga and Elliott (1987), p. 215.
16. Ibid., p. 219.
17. *Minneapolis Star and Tribune* (1987).
18. Krisberg, Litsky, and Schwartz (1984), pp. 159–62.
19. U.S. Department of Justice, Bureau of Justice Statistics (1985), p. 416.
20. U.S. Department of Justice, Bureau of Justice Statistics (1983), p. 33.
21. Strasberg (1984), p. 22.
22. U.S. Deparment of Justice, Bureau of Justice Statistics (1985), p. 416.
23. Ibid., p. 439.
24. Elliott, Ageton, and Huizinga (undated), p. 2-61.
25. Ibid., p. 2-60.
26. Wolfgang (1987) pp. 17–18.
27. Hamparian et al. (1984), p. 5.
28. Ibid., p. 26.
29. Cook and Lamb (1986), p. 220.

References

Cook, P.J., and Laub, J.M. 1986. "The (Surprising) Stability of Youth Crime Rates." *Journal of Quantitative Criminology* 2(3): 265–77.

Elliott, D.S.; Ageton, S.S.; and Huizinga, D. Undated. *The Social Correlates of Delinquent Behavior: 1976–1980*. Boulder, Colo.: Behavioral Research Institute.

Hamparian, D.M.; Davis, J.M.; Jacobson, J.M.; and McGrow, R.E. 1984. *The Young Criminal Years of the Violent Few*. Cleveland, Ohio: Federation for Community Planning.

Hindelang, M.J., and McDermott, M.J. 1981. *Analysis of National Crime Victimization Survey Data to Study Serious Delinquent Behavior (Monograph Two)—Juvenile Criminal Behavior: An Analysis of Rates and Victim Characteristics*. New York: Criminal Justice Research Center.

Huizinga, D., and Elliott, D.S. 1987. "Juvenile Offenders Prevalence, Offender Incidence and Arrest Rates by Race." *Crime and Delinquency* 33(2): 206–23.

John Howard Association. 1982. *Juvenile Crime in Cook County: A Wave or a Ripple?* Chicago: John Howard Association.

Krisberg, B.; Litsky, P.; and Schwartz, I.M. 1984. "Youth in Confinement: Justice by Geography." *Journal of Research in Crime and Delinquency* 21(2): 153–81.

Minneapolis Star and Tribune. 19 February 1987. "State Ranks High in Jailing Juveniles."

Opinion Research Corporation. 1982. *Public Attitudes Toward Youth Crime*. Minneapolis: University of Minnesota, Hubert H. Humphrey Institute of Public Affairs.

Regnery, A.S. 1985. "Getting Away with Murder: Why the Juvenile Justice System Needs an Overhaul." Reprint from *Policy Review* 34.

Strasberg, P.A. 1984. "Recent National Trends in Serious Juvenile Crime." In *Violent Juvenile Offenders: An Anthology*, ed. R.A. Mathias, P. DeMuro, and R.S. Allinson, pp. 5–30. Hackensack, New Jersey: National Council on Crime and Delinquency.

U.S. Department of Justice, Bureau of Justice Statistics. 1983. *Report to the Nation on Crime and Justice: The Data*. Washington, D.C.: U.S. Government Printing Office.

———. 1985. *Sourcebook of Criminal Justice Statistics*. Washington, D.C.: U.S. Government Printing Office.

———. May 1986. *Criminal Victimization in the United States, 1984*. Washington, D.C.: U.S. Government Printing Office.

U.S. Department of Justice, Federal Bureau of Investigation. *Part I and Part II Offenses*. Data tape. Washington, D.C.: Federal Bureau of Investigation.

Wolfgang, M.E. 1987. "Youth Crime: Sumer and Later."In *Violent Juvenile Crime: What Do We Know About It and What Can We Do About It?* ed. L. Eddison, pp. 7–22. Minneapolis: University of Minnesota, Center for the Study of Youth Policy.

3

The Politics of Juvenile Corrections

GREAT things were expected to happen after the Juvenile Justice and Delinquency Prevention Act of 1974 was passed. The reformers envisioned that hundreds of thousands of juveniles would be diverted from the juvenile justice system, that detention and training populations would be cut by 50 percent or more, that the practice of jailing juveniles would be ended (or largely curtailed), and that the quality of justice for children would improve significantly.

It has been more than ten years since the act was passed. More than $1 billion in federal juvenile crime prevention and control funds has been spent. The sparse existing data suggest, however, that the results have fallen far short of the hopes of the child advocates and the authors of the legislation. There has been some progress in removing children from adult jails—a topic that will be discussed in greater detail later. However, hardly any progress has been made in stemming the flow of youth into the juvenile courts.[1] Also, serious questions are being raised about just how much the quality of justice for children has improved; and the juvenile detention and corrections industry is flourishing.

The Hennepin County Experience: A Case in Point

A few years ago, a domed stadium was built in Minneapolis. It was built on a parcel of land that had once housed the fifty-four-bed Hennepin County Juvenile Detention Center. The decision to construct the stadium where the detention center had been located triggered an all-too-familiar process in the planning of juvenile institutions—a process that pitted the voices of reason and rationality against the "juvenile crime fighters."

Those interested in a rational planning process included some of the professional planners who worked for the county, a handful of county administrative officials, and a couple of county board members. They were interested in youth population and juvenile crime projections. They wanted to know what impact various detention admissions criteria might have on public safety and on the number of secure beds that would be needed. They consulted with experts in the field, reviewed relevant research findings, and examined the experiences in other jurisdictions.

This group concluded that the county could get by with as few as sixty-three secure detention beds. They wanted to locate the facility in or near the neighborhood from which the bulk of the admissions came. They favored such a site because land values were cheaper there than in downtown Minneapolis and because this might be a factor in keeping the number of admissions down. They thought that a neighborhood site would facilitate returning more youth to their parents or guardians for supervision pending their appearance in court. They felt it would be easier to find a neighborhood site that would allow for adequate outdoor recreation and public parking. Also, they wanted to put courtrooms and probation offices in the facility so that they would be more accessible to the community.

The "juvenile crime fighters," who were advocating for a 125- to 150-bed facility, included the chief juvenile court judge, juvenile probation officers, detention center staff, prosecutors, and law enforcement officials. They wanted a larger facility because the juvenile crime rate was expected to increase when the "echo baby boomers" reached their teens. The juvenile court judge argued that more juveniles would be held in detention because the juvenile justice system was becoming more "punishment-oriented" and that juveniles needed to be held "accountable" for their behavior. Never mind the fact that the detention center is intended for preadjudication (pretrial) purposes and that the youth confined have not yet been found guilty.

The chief juvenile court judge traveled around the county trying to whip up support for a bigger facility. He spoke to law enforcement groups, the county criminal justice advisory committee, neighborhood associations, and community groups. He told them that a bigger detention center would be an effective crime control measure and encouraged them to write letters to county politicians.

The "juvenile crime fighters" wanted the detention center to be built downtown. Prosecutors and public defenders wanted it close to their offices, because it would be too inconvenient to have to travel to see their clients or to prosecute cases. At a public hearing on the issue, a juvenile court referee raised a number of concerns, including the fact that there weren't any "trendy restaurants" near the neighborhood sites being considered. Some detention center staff members were concerned because a site outside the downtown area would deny the staff access to downtown department stores during the noon hour.

The three years of bickering over the size and location pushed the price tag up by more than 40 percent. The skyrocketing costs forced a hasty compromise, and the county board eventually approved the construction of an 87-bed facility. The detention center was built on a relatively small site in close proximity to other county buildings in downtown Minneapolis. It has limited outdoor recreation space and no public parking. Parents and visitors have to use metered parking spaces on the streets or pay to park in nearby parking facilities. The building, called the Hennepin County Juvenile Justice Center, houses juvenile courtrooms and juvenile probation offices. The detention center portion is the most physically secure institution of its kind in the United States.

The number of annual admissions has been increasing since the day the doors were opened. On several occasions, the number of youth confined exceeded the capacity. In 1986, 3,175 juveniles were admitted to the facility. Less than one-third were accused of committing Part I violent or property crimes. The overwhelming majority were incarcerated for misdemeanors; various probation, rule, and technical violations; absconding from a court-ordered placement; failure to appear in court for a scheduled hearing; running away; or curfew violations. A number of the juveniles admitted were 11 years of age or younger; one was 5 years old.[2]

The facility ended up costing more than $16 million to build. The operating budget for 1986 was $3,100,716. Because of budget cuts during fiscal year 1987–88, four of the six teachers were laid off. As a result, juveniles in detention spend only two hours a day in classes.

An elected public official who was intimately involved in the building process summed up the experience: "The project started out with an optimum number of choices. Each step of the process chipped away at the best choices until we were left with the worst options possible."

The new domed stadium was named the Hubert H. Humphrey Metrodome. The late vice-president and senator from Minnesota would probably not approve of the stadium being named after him if he would have known it resulted in the building of a bigger lock-up for kids.

Changing Patterns of Incarceration

Juvenile incarceration trends are usually examined by tracking the numbers and rates of annual admissions to detention centers and training schools as well as the numbers and rates of youth confined in these facilities on a particular day. The "get tough" movement that swept the country in the late 1970s and early 1980s had a significant impact on the numbers and rates of youth confined and on how these institutions are being used. The impact on the institutions was so great that the traditional approaches to examining incarceration trends have become obsolete. To get an accurate picture of youth detention and correctional policies and practices today, it is essential that the numbers and rates of juveniles confined annually and at any one time be disaggregated by type of incarceration and by type of facility. The reason this must be done is that detention centers and training schools in many jurisdictions are no longer used only for the purposes for which they were originally intended. In fact, many of these facilities have undergone so much change that the traditional labels used to describe them don't seem to fit anymore.

Detention centers are high-security institutions. They are supposed to house juveniles on a predispositional status who are awaiting their appearance in court and, to a much lesser extent, juveniles who are awaiting transfer to another placement after disposition of their cases.

Today, detention centers in nearly half of the states are being used for commitment purposes as well. As indicated in table 3–1, 18,977 juveniles were committed to juvenile detention centers in 1984. These youth now comprise more than 9 percent of the nearly 14,000

Table 3–1
COMMITMENTS TO DETENTION CENTERS, 1984

State	Number of Commitments	Rate per 100,000	Average Length of Stay (days)
Washington	5,076	985.6	12.1
California	7,560	259.6	32.9
Colorado	567	152.4	25.0
Nebraska	248	129.2	13.0
Indiana	690	99.6	30.1
Tennessee	548	94.8	3.0
Illinois	1,068	87.8	58.8
Kentucky	403	85.7	9.5
Alabama	437	85.7	14.9
Ohio	1,109	83.6	19.3
South Dakota	44	50.6	50.4
Michigan	466	45.9	74.9
Alaska	14	21.9	318.1
Georgia	135	20.7	70.5
West Virginia	48	19.5	45.4
Texas	297	16.8	61.9
North Carolina	60	10.7	304.2
Louisiana	58	10.1	25.0
Nevada	10	9.4	32.4
Missouri	27	5.2	110.2
Florida	60	5.2	60.8
Massachusetts	25	4.3	212.9
New Jersey	21	2.3	46.4
Minnesota	6	1.2	74.8
National totals	18,977	71.2	28.9

Source: U.S. Census Bureau, *Children in Custody.* Washington, D.C. 1985.

juveniles locked up in detention centers on any one given day. In 1984, they accounted for approximately 5 percent of the 408,128 juveniles admitted to detention centers and for more than 10 percent of the more than five million days of detention.

As can be seen in the table, although the average length of stay for youth committed to detention centers is approximately thirty days, juveniles committed to these facilities in some states are confined for substantial periods of time. For instance, the average length of stay for juveniles in such states as Missouri, North Carolina, Massachusetts, and Alaska are as long as or longer than the average lengths of stay in training schools in some states. Youth corrections officials in Massachusetts are troubled by this practice and have recently taken steps to end it.

Training schools are supposed to be for juveniles committed by the courts after they have been adjudicated (found guilty). With the exception of Massachusetts and Utah—states with small, high-security treatment units—these institutions tend to be large, campus-type, congregate care facilities located outside large cities or in rural areas. In 1984, 15 percent of the total annual admissions to training schools were for predispositional purposes (for example, for preadjudication detention and for diagnosis and assessment).

Table 3–2 lists the states where juveniles were reported to have been admitted to training schools on some type of predispositional status in 1984. A few states—such as Maine, Rhode Island, and New Hampshire—have no detention centers. Because of this, the training schools in those states have historically served multiple functions. The one training school in Alaska also doubles as a detention facility. However, this is not the case in the remaining states or in the District of Columbia. Maryland has the highest number of detainees admitted to training schools. Approximately 70 percent of all admissions to Maryland's training schools are detainees, even though there are a number of detention centers in the state.

What is particularly interesting is the fact that the average length of

Table 3–2
PREDISPOSITIONAL ADMISSIONS TO TRAINING SCHOOLS, 1984

State	Number of Admissions	Rate per 100,000	Average Length of Stay (days)
Alaska	1,420	2,218.8	14.0
District of Columbia	665	1,090.2	59.2
Maryland	2,648	506.3	22.1
New Hampshire	502	418.3	30.0
Rhode Island	290	261.3	30.0
Maine	331	228.3	13.0
Nebraska	429	223.4	21.7
Minnesota	813	161.6	11.8
Indiana	498	71.9	16.3
New Mexico	64	34.4	84.0
New Jersey	283	31.2	11.0
Missouri	131	25.3	30.3
Wyoming	4	5.7	14.0
California	105	3.6	15.5
Kentucky	7	1.4	1.0
National totals	8,190	30.7	22.8

Source: U.S. Census Bureau, *Children in Custody.* Washington, D.C. 1985.

stay for juveniles confined on a predispositional status in training schools is relatively long—almost twice as long as for juveniles similarly confined in detention centers. It is about 80 percent as long as the average length of stay for juveniles committed to detention centers.

The mix of pre- and postadjudication populations now found in these facilities indicates that both must be examined carefully in order to map trends more accurately and to examine the development and impact of youth detention and correctional policies on the national, state, and local levels. For example, if we want to get an accurate picture of the number and rate of juveniles committed to "training schools" nationally and in each state, it is essential to take into account those youth who are committed to serve time in juvenile detention centers, particularly in view of some of the long average lengths of stay. Table 3–3 ranks the states according to their rate of commitment to both training schools and detention centers in 1984. Washington state emerges as having the highest commitment rate in the nation. Washington leads the rest of the states because more than four times as many juveniles are committed to local county-operated juvenile detention centers as to state-administered training schools. If only the commitments to training schools were counted, Washington would drop down to seventeenth in the national rankings.

Table 3–3

COMMITMENTS TO DETENTION CENTERS AND
TRAINING SCHOOLS, 1984

Ranking	State	Number of Admissions	Rate per 100,000
1	Washington	6,239	1,211
2	District of Columbia	406	666
3	Oregon	1,897	600
4	California	15,463	531
5	Arizona	1,972	518
6	Wyoming	273	390
7	Tennessee	2,192	379
8	Montana	376	365
9	Ohio	4,656	351
10	Delaware	234	325
11	Minnesota	1,617	321
12	Maine	453	312
13	Indiana	2,091	302
14	Alaska	186	291

Table 3–3 continued
COMMITMENTS TO DETENTION CENTERS AND TRAINING SCHOOLS, 1984

Ranking	State	Number of Admissions	Rate per 100,000
15	Nevada	300	283
16	Nebraska	539	281
17	Colorado	931	250
18	New Mexico	458	246
19	Illinois	2,871	236
20	Alabama	1,179	231
21	Maryland	1,199	229
22	South Carolina	842	228
23	New Hampshire	269	224
24	Virginia	1,444	216
25	North Dakota	184	216
26	Kansas	452	214
27	Georgia	1,299	200
28	Mississippi	707	197
29	North Carolina	1,037	185
30	Kentucky	867	184
31	South Dakota	157	180
32	Rhode Island	188	170
33	Hawaii	204	169
34	West Virginia	412	167
35	Iowa	574	161
36	Louisiana	886	154
37	New Jersey	1,389	153
38	Arkansas	440	149
39	Texas	2,629	149
40	Wisconsin	770	130
41	Michigan	1,062	105
42	Connecticut	279	102
43	Missouri	506	98
44	Idaho	122	90
45	Florida	983	86
46	New York	1,217	81
47	Utah	180	77
48	Oklahoma	215	55
49	Pennsylvania	709	51
50	Massachusetts[a]	25	4
51	Vermont[b]	0	0
	National totals	65,580	245

Source: U.S. Census Bureau, *Children in Custody*. Washington, D.C. 1985.
[a] Officials in Massachusetts did not report the number of commitments to their small, high-security treatment units to the Census Bureau for 1984.
[b] Vermont does not have a training school facility.

In 1978, lawmakers in Washington enacted "just deserts" model juvenile code. One of the unique features of the law was its emphasis on mandatory and determinant sentencing. At the time it was enacted, policymakers and juvenile justice professionals in Washington and throughout the country heralded it as a major advance. Clearly, the law—which allows for short-term commitments to detention centers—is weighted heavily on the "deserts" and has catapulted Washington into the lead in sentencing juveniles to publicly operated juvenile detention centers and training schools by a substantial margin over its closest competitor.

The same applies to detention centers. The only way to get an accurate picture of the number of juveniles being incarcerated pending their appearance in court is to count those being confined on a predispositional status in training schools. Table 3–4 ranks the states by their rates of incarceration of juveniles for predispositional purposes in both detention centers and training schools. Because of the high volume of admissions to detention centers, the rankings of the states do not differ significantly when juveniles detained in training schools are taken into account. However, there is an impact on a state such as Maryland, in which 38 percent of the juveniles detained in the state are confined in training schools.

It is interesting to note that seven of the ten states with the highest rates of predispositional incarceration are western states.

Table 3–4
PREDISPOSITIONAL ADMISSIONS TO DETENTION
CENTERS AND TRAINING SCHOOLS, 1984

Ranking	State	Number of Admissions	Rate per 100,000
1	District of Columbia	5,549	9,097
2	Nevada	5,228	4,932
3	New Mexico	6,686	3,595
4	California	104,387	3,585
5	Alaska	2,193	3,427
6	Washington	15,501	3,010
7	Florida	28,205	2,455
8	Arizona	8,496	2,230
9	Colorado	8,207	2,206
10	Hawaii	2,659	2,198
11	Ohio	27,593	2,079

Table 3–4 continued
PREDISPOSITIONAL ADMISSIONS TO DETENTION CENTERS AND TRAINING SCHOOLS, 1984

Ranking	State	Number of Admissions	Rate per 100,000
12	Georgia	13,119	2,015
13	Utah	4,506	1,926
14	Tennessee	11,071	1,915
15	Oregon	5,270	1,668
16	Missouri	7,991	1,546
17	South Dakota	1,339	1,539
18	Indiana	10,515	1,517
19	Texas	24,720	1,398
20	Maryland	6,932	1,325
21	Virginia	8,656	1,298
22	Minnesota	6,371	1,267
23	Kansas	2,476	1,173
24	Delaware	787	1,093
25	Illinois	13,240	1,089
26	Nebraska	1,917	998
27	Mississippi	3,501	978
28	Pennsylvania	11,721	842
29	Michigan	7,940	782
30	New Jersey	6,976	770
31	Alabama	3,874	760
32	Idaho	852	631
33	Kentucky	2,752	586
34	Louisiana	3,241	562
35	North Carolina	3,114	556
36	Wisconsin	3,289	554
37	Connecticut	1,425	552
38	Oklahoma	1,806	461
39	North Dakota	373	439
40	New Hampshire	502	418
41	Arkansas	1,231	417
42	Iowa	1,337	376
43	New York	5,353	356
44	West Virginia	862	350
45	Massachusetts	1,794	309
46	South Carolina	1,068	289
47	Rhode Island	290	261
48	Maine	331	228
49	Wyoming	4	6
50	Vermont	0	0
51	Montana	0	0
	National totals	397,250	1,413

Source: U.S. Census Bureau, *Children in Custody.* Washington, D.C. 1985.

Incarceration of Minority Youth

The "get tough" movement also had a significant impact on the racial makeup of the juveniles confined in institutions. Since 1977, there has been a substantial increase in the number and proportion of minority youth confined in detention centers and training schools all around the country. In fact, minority youth now comprise approximately 50 percent of all the juveniles confined in publicly operated juvenile detention and correctional facilities in the United States. Black males are overrepresented by almost 180 percent in comparison to their numbers in the general population, and Hispanic males are overrepresented by 86 percent.[3] In contrast, 65 percent of the youth showing up in private youth detention and correctional facilities are white. This suggests that a racially segregated system of youth corrections may be evolving in the United States, a system in which black, hispanic, and native American youth are ending up in public institutions and whites are in private facilities.

The overrepresentation of minority youth is commonly explained by the fact that minorities account for a disproportionate amount of the *arrests* for serious juvenile crime. Although this is true, as mentioned earlier, it is not necessarily true that minority youth account for a substantially disproportionate amount of the serious juvenile *crime* that is committed. The fact that minority juvenile offenders are at greater risk of being apprehended than white youth who commit similar crimes is more than likely one of the critical factors accounting for the extraordinary high rates of incarceration of minority youth.

In the Matter of California

It is considered impolite to single out or seem to pick on one particular state. Nonetheless, it is impossible to ignore California's juvenile detention and correctional policies and their impact on the rest of the country.

California, a state that has only about 11 percent of the eligible youth population, accounts for 25 percent of all juveniles confined in public juvenile detention and correctional facilities (that is, detention centers, shelters, training schools, halfway houses, group homes, ranches, and camps) on a given day. California confines more juveniles in such institutions at any one time than the states of Illinois, Indiana, Iowa, Kansas, Michigan, Minnesota, Missouri, Nebraska, North Dakota, Ohio, South Dakota, and Wisconsin combined. California incarcerates more than twice the number on a given day than the states of Connecticut, Maine, Massachusetts, New Hampshire, New Jersey, New York, Pennsylvania, and Rhode Island combined.[4]

California accounts for approximately 16 percent of all juveniles confined on a given day in public training schools. In 1984, juveniles committed to the state were locked up for 2,660,188 days in California Youth Authority institutions. This was 23 percent of the 11,534,228 days served in training schools by youth across the country.

Approximately 35 percent of all youth confined on any given day in juvenile detention centers across the United States are locked up in California. As indicated in table 3–5, California accounted for 36 percent of all detention days in 1984. Compared to the rest of the nation, California's total detention days made up more than half of the total days of all other states and the District of Columbia combined.

One of the most dramatic examples of California's impact on the rest of the country can be seen in the data on commitments to detention. As indicated in table 3–6, the national rate of commitments to detention centers increased dramatically between 1977 and 1982 and then declined slightly between 1982 and 1984. The increase in the national rates between 1977 and 1979 was due

Table 3–5

DAYS OF DETENTION, CALIFORNIA AND ALL OTHER JURISDICTIONS, 1984

	National		California		All Other Jurisdictions	
	Number	Percent	Number	Percent	Number	Percent
Days of detention	5,089,852[a]	100	1,810,841	36	3,279,011	64
Days for detainees	4,536,605	100	1,562,377	34	2,974,228	66
Days for committed youth	548,446	100	248,464	45	299,982	55

Source: U.S. Census Bureau, Children in Custody. Washington, D.C. 1985.
[a] Days of detention total includes 4,801 days for juveniles admitted on a "voluntary" basis.

Table 3–6
COMMITMENT RATES TO DETENTION CENTERS, UNITED STATES AND CALIFORNIA, 1977–84

| | *Rate per 100,000* | | | |
	1977	1979	1982	1984
National	16.5	46.3	76.2	71.2
California excluded	13.4	12.4	44.4	48.1
California only	43.1	334.3	339.9	259.6

Source: U.S. Census Bureau, *Children in Custody.* Washington, D.C. 1985.

entirely to the increase in commitments to detention centers in California. As can be seen, with California excluded, the national rates declined during that period. Similarly, the decline in the national rates between 1982 and 1984 was essentially due to the drop in commitments to detention centers in California. With California excluded from the national picture, the national rates continued upward.

This extraordinary situation in California did not develop overnight. In 1975, Allen L. Breed, then director of the California Youth Authority (CYA), released a study entitled *Hidden Closets: A Study of Detention Practices in California.* The study, which was conducted by George Saleeby, the CYA's deputy director, was an eye-opening account of the detention system in a state that was recognized during the 1960s for enlightened policies and was considered by many to be the standard-bearer in the field.

Saleeby found "California's system of juvenile halls, the largest and most secure in the nation . . . needlessly bulging with children as a result of consistent overuse and abuse of detention." He found that "35 percent of the children [were] released within 24 hours." This raised serious questions about "why they were detained in the first place." Moreover, Saleeby found that "criminal justice officials believe[d] more, not fewer, children should be detained." He concluded that the system was so entrenched that "change[s] in detention practices . . . [would] have to come from without, rather than from within, the system."[5]

In 1980, John Poulin and his colleagues at the University of Chicago conducted a national study of juvenile detention and jailing practices during the mid-1970s. They found the number of juveniles detained in California to be so "extreme" in comparison to the rest of the country that they also singled it out for special consideration. They concluded: "There is no way to reduce the use of secure detention in the United States to a reasonable level without affecting its misuse in California."[6] This assessment is still true today.

The picture that emerges shows California leading the pack as one of the most (if not the most) punishing states for children in the country. Also, as noted in chapter 1, California officials cannot even guarantee the safety of their wards. One wonders how a state that was once considered one of the most innovative and enlightened jurisdictions in the country managed to sink so low. More important, given the magnitude and the depth of the problem confronting the state, one wonders whether California will ever emerge as a leader again.

Limited Benefits of Incarceration

There are 404 detention centers and 190 training schools in the United States. They cost taxpayers more than $1 billion to operate each year. The question that must continually be asked is: Is the public getting the best return on its investment? There are growing doubts about whether this is the case. The same public opinion poll that indicated that most citizens believed the country to be in the midst of a serious juvenile crime wave also revealed that only 57 percent of those surveyed believed that shipping kids off "to correctional institutions serves as a deterrent to other youths for committing crimes."[7]

There is growing evidence that these public doubts about the benefits of incarceration are well founded. Barry Krisberg and his colleagues at the National Council on Crime and Delinquency and the University of Minnesota's Humphrey Institute explored the enormous variation in rates of admissions to detention centers and training schools that occurs from state to state. Their analysis revealed that admission rates were largely unrelated to serious juvenile violent and property crime rates. The one variable they examined that accounted for more variation in rates than any other was the availability of beds.[8]

There is also mounting evidence that incarcerating juveniles in large congregate care institutions simply is not cost-effective. Recent scandals in Maryland's youth correctional facilities prompted officials to study the feasibility of closing the Montrose School, a 212-bed combination juvenile detention and commitment facility. The school has a $9.3 million budget and an annual per youth cost of $42,400.[9] Using data from fiscal years 1983–85, the officials found that "85 percent of [the] youth committed to Montrose were either re-referred to the Juvenile Services Administration [the state corrections agency] or re-adjudicated within two years of their first admission."[10] Maryland's other youth correctional institution, the Hickey School, isn't much better. Almost three-quarters of the youth released from the Hickey School in 1983 were returned to the facility within two years.[11]

Officials in Florida recently conducted a follow-up study of juveniles released from the state's two large training schools. The findings indicate that a sample of 303 youth released from the institutions in 1984 had a 60 percent recidivism rate within just one year.[12]

These same dismal statistics are now showing up for juveniles committed to adult prisons. In a report prepared for former Florida governor Robert Graham during the last days of his administration, researchers found that 60 percent of a sample of juveniles released from Florida's prisons in 1980 were recommitted to the adult prison system within four years. The report noted that the recidivism rate was far higher for juveniles than for adults.[13]

Research from California is equally sobering. A ten-year follow-up study of juveniles released from selected California Youth Authority institutions indicated that 80 percent were rearrested for having committed serious crimes.[14]

The Quiet Revolution

Elected public officials, public interest groups, and juvenile justice professionals in a growing number of states are starting to seriously reexamine youth detention and correctional policies in their jurisdictions. This is not happening simply because they are realizing that there is a more cost-effective way of tackling the juvenile crime problem. It is happening because the costs for maintaining institutional programs are high—and states are confronted with serious financial problems—and because of litigation over abusive practices and unconstitutional conditions of confinement. Once prompted to make changes, a number of states are choosing to replicate the reforms undertaken in Massachusetts and Utah, two states recognized for their enlightened and effective approaches.

In 1972, Jerry Miller, then commissioner of the Department of Youth Services in Massachusetts, closed that state's large training schools. When Miller first took over the scandal-ridden youth corrections system, he had no intention of closing the institutions. Miller, who had served as a psychiatric social worker in the armed services, first tried to "reform" the reform schools. He wanted to turn them into therapeutic communities where youth could be rehabilitated. He quickly learned that many of the staff members working in the institutions were too entrenched and actively resisted efforts to change. Consequently, Miller closed the institutions. Although the process was chaotic in the beginning—mainly because it happened quickly and because community-based alternatives were in short supply or simply didn't exist—the long-term results are impressive.

The Massachusetts youth corrections system has 171 secure treatment beds. They are located in twelve fifteen- to twenty-bed units strategically located throughout the state. There is a wide array of highly structured and credible community-based programs that allow for individualized programming. Also, 50 percent of the State Youth Corrections Agency's $48 million annual budget is contracted out to private, nonprofit vendors who deliver the bulk of the community-based services. The state also administers eight secure detention programs that have a total bed capacity of 128.[15]

A ten-year study of the Massachusetts reforms by researchers from the Harvard Center for Criminal Justice concluded that the "regions that most adequately implemented the reform measures with a diversity of programs did produce decreases in recidivism over time, as did those programs reflecting a higher degree of normalization on the institutionalization-normalization continuum."[16] Moreover, the closing of the training schools did not unleash a wave of serious juvenile crime. In fact, the rates of serious juvenile crime declined in Massachusetts, just as they have in other states throughout the country. Edward Loughran, the current commissioner of the Massachusetts Division of Youth Services, reports:

- The number of juveniles who graduate from the Division of Youth Services and end up in the state's adult prison system has dropped significantly. In 1972, 35 percent of the adults committed to the state prison system were graduates from the juvenile system. In 1985, only 15 percent had been through the juvenile system.
- The number of juveniles waived to adult courts has plummeted. In 1973, there were 129 juveniles waived to the adult courts in Massachusetts. Only 12 were waived in 1985.
- As of December 1986, only 36 juveniles were placed out-of-state.[17]

When Scott Matheson became governor of Utah, he inherited a lawsuit. The suit was against the Utah State Industrial School—a large, 450-bed institution located at the base of the Wasatch Mountains in Ogden, Utah. Despite the picturesque, campus-type setting and the constructive Mormon influence in the state, the State Industrial School was one of the most brutal and inhumane institutions of its kind in the country. In fact, Governor Matheson once commented that the practices in the institution, later known as the Youth Development Center, amounted to nothing less than "state-sanctioned abuse."

An assistant attorney general who represented the state in the litigation negotiated a consent decree and advised Matheson to sign it. Although he felt that the allegations in the lawsuit were accurate, Matheson refused to sign the decree because he didn't feel that it was appropriate to turn the management of the institution over to the federal court. He told the assistant attorney general to inform the federal judge that it was the responsibility of Utah's governor to make the institution a decent and safe place. Otherwise, the federal court should punish the state for not making it so.

Matheson appointed a blue-ribbon task force and charged them with the responsibility of reviewing Utah's entire criminal and juvenile justice systems. The task force looked into how juvenile offenders were handled in the state, heard testimony from experts in the field, and visited programs in other states. After a careful and time-consuming process, the task force recommended that Utah follow Massachusetts' lead and close its Youth Development Center.

Currently, there are two thirty-bed and one ten-bed high-security treatment units in Utah for violent juvenile offenders and youth who are chronic repeaters. Youth corrections officials in Utah developed a diverse network of highly structured, community-based programs for all other youth committed to the state. The community-based programs are primarily run by private vendors under contract with the state. A substantial proportion of the funds for the community-based programs came from monies that used to support the Youth Development Center. Some of the funds used for the construction of the two small units came from the sale of state land that surrounded the old Youth Development Center.

The Utah system was recently evaluated by the National Council on Crime and Delinquency (NCCD). The NCCD researchers found that the youth who were committed to the Division of Youth Corrections and placed in community-based programs had dramatic declines in their rates of reoffending—declines that the researchers believed to be greater than what could be explained by maturation or other similar factors.[18] The researchers concluded: "Utah's policy of community-based corrections did not worsen public safety."[19] They also concluded that "the imposition of appropriate community-based controls in highly active serious and chronic juvenile offenders is consistent with public protection goals."[20]

The study findings also indicated that Utah's youth corrections policies make good sense from an economic perspective. If the juvenile offenders committed to the state were institutionalized instead of being placed in well-structured, community-based programs, the state would have had to make a one-time expenditure of $32.5 million in construction funds and would have to shell out approximately $10 million each year in annual operating costs.[21]

Utah is not the only state where major reforms are being implemented. Oklahoma's juvenile justice statutes have been over-hauled, and three of that state's five youth training schools have been closed. Since 1979, training school populations have been cut in half in Arkansas and Idaho and by nearly 40 percent in Missouri. Policymakers in Colorado are in the process of implementing a number of sweeping youth corrections reforms; a central part of the package includes development of community-based alternatives and plans to reduce the number of training school beds from 354 to 255 by 1989. Oregon officials have reduced their training school popu-lations and are considering closing the McLaren School for Boys, the largest juvenile correctional facility in the state. They are interested in the prospect of freeing up the more than $8 million that goes into running the institution annually to finance community-based alternatives. Policymakers and youth corrections officials in Virginia and Georgia are exploring ways to expand community-based programs, with an eye toward reducing the number of training school beds and, if possible, closing some facilities.

Youth corrections officials in Maryland recently closed the infamous Montrose School and are moving to reduce the population in the state's one other training school. Also, they are exploring ways to cut down on the high numbers of juveniles who are waived each year to the adult criminal courts and who end up in the adult prison system. Youth corrections officials in West Virginia closed down that state's one large juvenile training school. Youth corrections officials in Louisiana are in the midst of reducing their state training school populations and are hoping to close a large institution for girls. Also, state lawmakers in Louisiana recently enacted legislation taking away the authority of the juvenile courts to determine where youth committed to the state should be placed and putting the responsibility for that decision in the hands of the Division of Youth Corrections. In Delaware, the governor, the attorney general, the chief judge of Family Court, and staff members of the state youth corrections agency are in the beginning stages of implementing a plan aimed at reducing the population at the antiquated Ferris School. Their goal is to expand the number and diversity of community-based programs and to try to limit the number of youth in secure care to about thirty-five or forty. Policymakers and professionals in North Dakota, Montana, Florida, Ohio, Tennessee, Maine, Wyoming, Nevada, Mississippi, South Carolina, Rhode Island, and Wisconsin are also in the process of reexamining and rethinking their approaches to juvenile law violators.

Juvenile Detention: An Area Ripe for Reform

Some of the same questions that are being raised about the wisdom of relying on training schools need to be raised about detention centers. The decision to confine a youth in a detention facility is an important one—one that various sets of national juvenile justice standards and the professional consensus agree should be exercised with caution.[22] The decision to detain is important because there is evidence that the inappropriate use of detention contributes to negative labeling of youth and may adversely affect subsequent decisions made about them by juvenile justice and other officials.[23] Nevertheless, there is considerable evidence that detention is used excessively throughout the country.

With the exception of only a handful of states, detention centers are locally administered and financed. County board members need to be made aware of the overwhelming evidence that detention is overused and that admissions to these facilities can be substantially reduced without appreciably increasing the risk to the community. They also need to understand that reasonable and prudent changes in detention policies and practices may help realize significant long-range cost savings.

Genessee County, Michigan, is a case in point. The county's population of about 430,000 people includes the economically and socially depressed city of Flint. In 1970, Judge Luke Quinn was appointed to the probate court and served on the juvenile bench. The court administered a seventy-two-bed juvenile detention center that was financed by the county board. The first year Judge Quinn took over as the juvenile court judge, 1,573 juveniles were locked up in the detention center. Approximately 50 percent of the youth confined were status offenders. Judge Quinn and his colleagues on the bench had serious questions about the appropriateness of many of the admissions. As a result, the court developed detention intake criteria that limited admissions to only those juveniles who presented a clear and substantial threat to the community, prohibited the detention of status offenders, and played a leadership role in the development and implementation of alternatives.

Admissions to the detention center dropped to the point at which it was no longer economically feasible for the county of operate the facility. In 1978, the county board turned the institution over to the state. It is now a regional facility that is operated and financed by the state. This transition resulted in a net savings of approximately $1 million each year for Genessee County taxpayers. In 1986, fewer than 250 of the admissions to the facility came from Genessee County.

Professor C. Ronald Huff of Ohio State University recently completed an evaluation of the home detention program implemented in Cuyahoga County (Cleveland), Ohio. This home detention program was started in 1981, primarily in response to an increasing detention population. Huff concluded: "The widespread implementation (and, where already existing, responsible expansion) of home detention programs in Ohio could significantly reduce the population of local juvenile detention centers in our state."[24]

Facts Don't Always Make a Difference

In light of the high costs and limited benefits of incarceration, one wonders why so many state and county policymakers and professionals continue to rely on it so heavily. The reasons have little or nothing to do with public safety or with controlling juvenile crime. Instead, they have to do with such issues as providing jobs, keeping the economy of some small community going, and giving the appearance of being "tough" on juvenile crime.

One of the most widely known secrets in juvenile justice circles in Washington state is that youth corrections officials have wanted to close down the Green Hill School for several years. The Green Hill School, a 162-bed training school built in 1891, is located in Chehalis, Washington, a small rural community in the southern part of the state. Green Hill has recently been cited for inadequate programming, abusive and unprofessional practices, and unconstitutional conditions.[25] Parts of the school are dilapidated, and it has been estimated that it would cost millions to remodel the facility in order to bring it up to minimum health, safety, fire, and programmatic standards. State youth corrections officials estimate that closing the facility could save approximately $10.5 million in operating expenditures over the next decade.[26] They have devised a plan to shut down the institution that would keep the number of employees forced out of jobs to a minimum.

Despite the compelling reasons to close the institution, Green Hill remains open. The state employees union and citizens who own or work in local businesses that depend on the state money spent in their community, or who have state contracts to deliver goods and services to the school, lobby hard to keep it open. Bureaucratic and political insiders acknowledge that the governor is sensitive to the economic impact the closing of the school would have on the community. As one official put it: "Our governor wants to be a two-term governor!"

The juvenile justice system in Washington state has been the subject of numerous studies and reports, most of which have had little or no impact in bringing about major reforms. Recently, staff members of the Washington State Department of Social and Health Services developed a ten-year youth corrections plan. The plan outlines two basic policy options for the state. One option emphasizes maintaining the status quo and keeping the number of training school beds at about the present level. The second option calls for shifting the emphasis toward community-based programs and substantially reducing the number of training school beds.[27] The hope of some juvenile justice and child welfare officials who have been advocating for reforms is that the policy option favoring community-based programs will be implemented after the upcoming gubernatorial election if the current governor is re-elected. Needless to say, it will be interesting to see what happens in Washington, particularly if the new governor stays in office.

In Arizona, two training schools are being built that aren't even needed. One is a 140-bed institution for boys; the other is a 120-bed facility for girls. They will cost millions to construct. The operating costs will run into the millions annually and will continue to grow in the decades ahead.

In 1982, Arizona ranked seventh in the country in its rate of incarceration of juveniles. By 1984, Arizona's ranking inched up to fifth. The recent increase in the training school admissions is largely the result of a doubling of commitments and parole revocations for girls and a doubling of the commitments for boys.

Close associates of former Arizona governor Bruce Babbitt acknowledge that his aspirations for national office adversely influenced his thinking about juvenile and adult corrections. They contend that Babbitt viewed corrections as a problem and a potential Achilles' heel. They maintain that, as a result, Babbitt pretty much went along with whatever the Department of Corrections and the legislature recommended, which was usually what was politically expedient.

It is interesting that in 1986, former governor Babbitt gave a major address at a national youth advocacy conference in which he "repeated his call for a national children's agenda that would bring liberals and conservatives together." As Babbitt perceived it:

> Such an agenda would be comprised of policies that [would] ensure:
> • day care for children of working mothers;
> • adequate health care for all children;
> • parental leave for working parents and would-be parents;
> • enforcement of child support payments;
> • teen-age pregnancy prevention.[27]

Evidently, Babbitt was unaware that policymakers in Massachusetts (Senator Edward Kennedy's home state) and in Utah (Senator Orrin Hatch's home state) have already implemented such approaches to handling juvenile offenders—with impressive results.

Discussion

The "get tough" policies that swept the country in the late 1970s and early 1980s had a significant impact on state and local youth detention and correctional policies. One of the major responses from politicians and juvenile justice professionals to public pressure to "do something" about the juvenile crime problem was to formalize and expand the practice of committing youth to detention centers. The result is that juvenile detention facilities in many jurisdictions are being used for purposes that make them virtually indistinguishable from adult jails; the only real difference between the two is the age of the populations they serve. Like jails, detention centers in nearly half the states are housing pre- and postadjudication populations. Because detention centers are not designed or built to house, keep separate, and provide adequate programming for these two differing populations, they are almost always comingled in these institutions. This is a practice that is condemned by knowledgeable professionals in the field, is contrary to the recommendations of all known and generally accepted professional juvenile justice standards, and is fraught with potential legal, administrative, and programmatic problems.

The large numbers of juveniles being confined in training schools for detention and precourt diagnostic purposes, coupled with their comparatively long average length of stay, suggest that many of these youth are being confined under conditions that essentially amount to predispositional punishment. Many of the juveniles placed in training schools for evaluation or diagnostic purposes are, in reality, sent to these places to give them "a taste of institutional life" in the hope that this will convince them to mend their ways. Moreover, the diagnostic workups that are prepared on the youth tend to be of little or no value. Most juvenile probation departments lack the resources to follow through on the recommendations contained in the reports. Also, many of the workups are based on the medical psychiatric model, a model that has proved to be largely ineffective in working with delinquent youth.

The "get tough" movement has also come down hard on the heads of minorities and has contributed heavily to the development of a youth detention and correctional system that is becoming increasingly racially segregated. There has been a significant increase in the proportion of minority youth confined in public juvenile detention and correctional institutions, while private facilities are populated mainly by whites. If this trend continues, it would not be unreasonable to expect the racial makeup in public detention centers and training schools eventually to mirror the populations in adult jails and state prison systems.

Fortunately, there is reason to believe that the "get tough" movement is waning and that we may be entering another new era of reform. It is apparent that policymakers and juvenile justice opinion leaders in a growing number of states—particularly in the West and the South, two regions of the country where one would least expect such developments to occur—are beginning to seriously reexamine their youth detention and correctional policies. Where this process is actively under way, they are generally adopting policies and strategies aimed at reducing reliance on incarceration in favor of increased use of highly structured and individualized community-based programs.

In addition, there is growing recognition and support for the notion that juvenile offenders who must be confined should be incarcerated in small high-security treatment units, units preferably with a maximum of fifteen to twenty beds. Large congregate-care training schools have no place in an enlightened and modern juvenile corrections system. Moreover, the recent experiences of the American Correctional Association (ACA) to find the "model" large juvenile training school should be a lesson to even the most ardent supporter of these relics. The ACA recently launched an effort to find the large public or privately operated juvenile training school that would serve as the "model" for the nation. They wanted to find the one or more institutions that would serve as an architectural and programmatic inspiration to all those who believed or wanted to believe in the benefits of these places. The ACA assembled a group of prominent youth correctional administrators to review the applications from facilities that were accredited by the National Commission on Accreditation for Corrections and were competing to be named the class of the field. After a lengthy review process, which included on-site visits to the facilities, the experts were unable to find one large youth correctional institution that they felt could be held up as a national model.[29]

Notes

1. Snyder, Hutzler, and Finnegan (1985), p. 9.
2. Hennepin County Bureau of Community Corrections (1987).
3. Krisberg et al.(1987), p. 186.
4. U.S. Department of Justice, Bureau of Justice Statistics (1986), p. 2.
5. Saleeby (1975), pp. 1–2.
6. Poulin et al. (1986), p. 53.
7. Opinion Research Corporation (1982).
8. Krisberg, Litsky, and Schwartz (1982), pp. 156–62.
9. Department of Health and Mental Hygiene (1986), p. 7.
10. Ibid., p. 3.
11. Florida Department of Health and Rehabilitative Services (1987), p. 9.
12. *Baltimore Evening Sun*, 4 April 1988.
13. Polivka (1986).
14. Greenwood et al. (1983), p. ix.
15. Massachusetts Department of Youth Services (1985), p. 11.
16. Coates, Miller, and Ohlin (1978), p. 177.
17. Loughran (1987), p. 18.
18. National Council on Crime and Delinquency (1987), p. 147.
19. Ibid.
20. Ibid.
21. Ibid., pp. 134–36.
22. Schwartz, Jackson-Beeck, and Anderson (1984), pp. 220–21.
23. Coates, Miller, and Ohlin (1978), p. 76.
24. Huff (1986), p. 13.
25. Lambert, D. 22 February 1988. Letter to author.

26. Shimpoch (1986).
27. Department of Social and Health Services (1988), pp. 10–17.
28. Fleming (1986), p. 5.
29. Schwartz (1988).

References

Baltimore Evening Sun. 25 April 1988. "Jail for Kids."

Coates, R.B.; Miller, A.D.; and Ohlin, L.E. 1978. *Diversity in a Youth Correctional System: Handling Delinquents in Massachusetts.* Cambridge, Mass.: Ballinger.

Department of Health and Mental Hygiene. 1986. *Feasibility and Desirability of Closing Montrose School.* Baltimore: Office of Planning and Policy Management.

Department of Social and Health Services. January 1988. *Division of Juvenile Rehabilitation Real Management Plan.* Olympia, Wash.: Department of Social and Health Services.

Fleming, D. 1986. "Child Advocacy Grows Up." *Youth Policy* 8 (11): 5–8.

Florida Department of Health and Rehabilitative Services. 1987 *A Preliminary Report on the Findings of Recidivism.* Tallahassee, Fla.: Children, Youth and Families Program Office Data Analysis Unit.

Greenwood, P.W.; Lipson, A.J.; Abrahamse, A.; and Zimring, F. June 1983. *Youth Crime and Juvenile Justice in California.* Santa Monica, Calif.: Rand Corporation.

Hennepin County Bureau of Community Corrections. 1987. *Hennepin County Juvenile Detention Center Annual Statistical Report.* Minneapolis: Hennepin County.

Huff, C.R. 1986. *Home Detention as a Policy Alternative for Ohio's Juvenile Courts: Executive Summary.* Columbus: Ohio State University, Program for the Study of Crime and Delinquency.

Huizinga, D., and Elliott, D.S. 1987. "Juvenile Offenders: Prevalence, Offender Incidence and Arrest Rates by Race." *Crime and Delinquency* 33 (2): 206–23.

Krisberg, B.; Litsky, P.; and Schwartz, I.M. 1982. *Youth in Confinement: Justice by Geography.* Minneapolis: University of Minnesota, Hubert H. Humphrey Institute of Public Affairs.

Krisberg, B.; Schwartz, I.M.; Fishman, G.; Eisikovits, Z.; Guttman, E.; and Joe, K. 1987. "The Incarceration of Minority Youth." *Crime and Delinquency* 33 (2): 173–205.

Lambert, D. 22 February 1988. Letter to author.

Loughran, E.J. 1987. "Juvenile Corrections: The Massachusetts Experience." In *Reinvesting Youth Corrections Resources: A Tale of Three States,* ed. L. Eddison, pp. 11–18. Minneapolis: University of Minnesota, Center for the Study of Youth Policy, Hubert H. Humphrey Institute of Public Affairs.

Massachusetts Department of Youth Services. 1985. *Annual Report.* Boston: Department of Youth Services, Public Information Office.

National Council on Crime and Delinquency. 1987. *The Impact of Juvenile Court Intervention.* San Francisco: National Council on Crime and Delinquency.

Office of Juvenile Justice and Delinquency Prevention. 1984. *Serious Juvenile Crime: A Redirected Federal Effort.* Washington, D.C.: U.S. Department of Justice.

Opinion Research Corporation. 1982. *Public Attitudes Toward Youth Crime.* Minneapolis: University of Minnesota, Hubert H. Humphrey Institute of Public Affairs.

Polivka, L. 1986. "Draft Report." State of Florida, Office of the Governor, Department of Planning and Budgeting. (Photocopy.)

Poulin, J.E.; Levitt, J.L.; Young, T.M.; and Pappenfort, D.M. 1986. *Juveniles in Detention Centers and Jails: An Analysis of State Variations During the Mid-1970s.* Washington, D.C.: U.S. Government Printing Office.

Saleeby, G. 1975. *Hidden Closets: A Study of Detention Practices in California.* Sacramento, Calif.: Department of Youth Authority.

Schwartz, I. 28 July 1988. Interview with Orlando Martinez.

Schwartz, I.M.; Jackson-Beeck, M.; and Anderson, R. 1984. "The 'Hidden' System of Juvenile Control." *Crime and Delinquency* 30 (3): 371–85.

Shimpoch, A.N. 7 February 1986. Memo to Orin C. Smith.

Snyder, H.N.; Hutzler, J.L.; and Finnegan, T.A. 1985. *Delinquency in the United States: 1982.* Pittsburgh, Pa.: National Center for Juvenile Justice.

U.S. Department of Justice, Bureau of Justice Statistics. 1985. *Children in Custody.* Washington, D.C.

4

The Jailing of Juveniles

W HEN it became known that President Jimmy Carter was going to appoint me administrator of the Office of Juvenile Justice and Delinquency Prevention (OJJDP), people called from all over the country offering advice. I received suggestions on everything from which programs I should fund to whom it would be good for me to know in Washington, D.C. The best advice came from a few close and trusted confidants. They told me not to let the job go to my head and not to think that I could change the world all at once. They urged that I choose one or two priority issues and concentrate on them. They also urged me to keep in mind that a presidential election was just over a year away, which meant that I might have only a limited amount of time to try to make a difference.

I decided that the one issue I really wanted to do something about was the problem of children in jail. Every year, hundreds of thousands of young people were being confined in adult jails and under some of the worst conditions imaginable. It was time to try to bring this shameful practice to an end.

I knew that the National Coalition for Jail Reform—a consortium of more than forty respected juvenile and criminal justice organizations, professional associations, and public interest groups—had a committee that was looking into this issue.[1] The committee chair, Don Jensen, was a fellow I had hired as a juvenile justice specialist when I was director of the John Howard Association in Chicago. I called Jensen and told him it seemed likely that I was going to be nominated by President Carter. I said that I hoped the coalition would develop a strong policy for the removal of juveniles from adult jails, because I wanted to try to make it a national priority and I knew their commitment to the issue would be extremely helpful.

My goal was simple. I wanted to get Congress to enact an amendment to the Juvenile Justice and Delinquency Prevention Act calling for the removal of juveniles from adult jails and police lockups. I also wanted Congress to declare that the states should move to accomplish this objective within a certain period of time or face the prospect of losing federal juvenile justice funds. I felt that an amendment was needed so that, in the event that there was a change in administration, the law would remain on the books. I also wanted a deadline, as I felt there would be little progress without one.

A Blow Is Struck for Kids

On the morning of March 19, 1980, I was sitting next to Charles B. Renfrew, the deputy attorney general of the United States, as he testified on the reauthorization of the Juvenile Justice and Delinquency Prevention Act before the Subcommittee on Human Resources of the Committee on Education and Labor of the U.S. House of Representatives. With deep conviction, Renfrew stated that the time had come to put an end to the practice of putting juveniles in adult jails and police lockups. He told the members of the subcommittee:

> [T]he jailing of children is harmful to them in several ways. The most widely-known harm is that of physical and sexual abuse by adults in the same facility. Even short-term, pre-trial or relocation detention exposes juveniles to assault, exploitation and injury.
>
> Sometimes, in an attempt to protect a child, local officials will isolate the child from contact with others. Because juveniles are highly vulnerable to emotional pressure, isolation of the type provided in adult facilities can have a long-term negative impact on an individual child's mental health.
>
> Having been built for adults who have committed criminal acts, jails do not provide an environment suitable for the care and maintenance of delinquent juveniles or status offenders. In addition, being treated like a prisoner reinforces a child's negative self-image. Even after release, a juvenile may be labeled as a criminal in his community as a result of his jailing, a stigma which can continue for a long period.
>
> The impact of jail on children is reflected by another grim

statistic—the suicide rate for juveniles incarcerated in adult jails during 1978 was approximately seven times the rate among children in secure juvenile detention facilities.

Renfrew added:

> I am pleased to note a growing number of court decisions which concur in this view. Placing children in jails has been found to violate their rights to treatment, to constitute a denial of due process, and to be cruel and unusual punishment. Some of these rulings have been far-reaching.

He concluded by asking that Congress both reauthorize the act and add an amendment that would call for the removal of juveniles from jails and police lockups.[2]

After hearing Renfrew's testimony, I was euphoric; it was one of the most exciting moments in my entire professional career. I was excited because this goal was about to be chiseled in legislative concrete and become reality.

My excitement diminished within a matter of weeks and eventually turned to frustration and disappointment when it appeared that no member of either the Subcommittee on Human Resources or the Committee on Education and Labor would author the amendment. Although no one said it directly, it was apparent that the amendment was perceived as controversial. There were concerns about how constituents back home—particularly judges and law enforcement officials—might react. There was an election coming up, and many members of Congress needed the support of these officials. Every congressional member I approached said that he or she would support such an amendment but would not be its author. Mark Davis, the OJJDP's congressional liaison, worked feverishly with congressional staffers, trying to encourage them to convince their bosses to author the bill. No one came forward. It was hard to fathom, but it appeared that this potentially historic piece of public policy was going to go by the wayside for lack of a sponsor.

About a month after Renfrew's testimony, one of my staff members was driving me to a meeting. He noticed that I was depressed and asked what was wrong. I told him that the jail amendment was going to die because we couldn't find a sponsor.

He told me he had a connection with Congressman Ray Kogovsek from Colorado, who was on the Committee on Education and Labor. He asked if it would be all right if he tried to arrange a meeting to see if Kogovsek would be willing to author the jail amendment. I told him to go ahead.

I should explain that this staff person had a knack for bungling assignments and causing problems. He had a tendency to give the impression that he had far more responsibility and influence than he really had. I had tried to "loan" this fellow out to other federal agencies as an easy way to get rid of him. Unfortunately, there were no takers. It seemed that everybody I talked to knew about him. When I couldn't get rid of him, I decided that I needed to keep close track of him.

One day I called him into my office. I told him that I was impressed with his expertise and experience in the field. I said that in order to get the maximum benefit from his advice and counsel, I was assigning him to work more closely with me. I indicated that I wanted him to accompany me to meetings and other important events. In essence, I made him my driver. He liked the idea because he could be seen with the administrator of the OJJDP. I liked the idea because I could keep an eye on him.

About a week later, we were sitting in Representative Kogovsek's office, talking to the congressman and one of his staff members about the jail amendment. I explained the Department of Justice position on the issue and why we felt that the amendment was important. His staff assistant asked a few questions and appeared to be supportive of our cause. Congressman Kogovsek didn't say much, but he listened carefully to what was being said. Near the end of the meeting, he looked at me and asked, "Is this the right thing to do?" I told him that it was. He tapped his pencil on the table and replied, "Let's do it."

A few weeks later, Kogovsek offered the amendment during a session of the Committee on Education and Labor and made a forceful and eloquent presentation on why it was important to remove juveniles from adult jails and police lockups. Florida Congressman Edward J. Stack, a former sheriff, also spoke on behalf of the amendment. It sailed through the committee without a dissenting vote and subsequently became the law of the land.

As I look back on that experience, I shudder to think that this important piece of child welfare legislation came about because of the personal contact made by an otherwise inept staff member in the Office of Juvenile Justice—a staff member I had earlier tried to get rid of.

The National Campaign to End the Practice of Jailing Juveniles

In the fall of 1973, the Senate Subcommittee to Investigate Juvenile Delinquency conducted a series of hearings on the jailing of juveniles. Among the first witnesses to testify for the subcommittee was Dr. Rosemary Sarri, one of the country's foremost authorities on juvenile justice. Sarri's testimony was a well-documented and shocking account of what was known about the problem and our inability to do much about it. Sarri told the subcommittee:

> An accurate portrait of the extent of juvenile jailing in the United States does not exist. Furthermore, it is difficult to develop one because of the lack of reliable and comparable information from the cities, counties, states and federal government.[3]

She also reported that "the jailing of juveniles occurs in both rural areas where available alternatives for custody of children are limited, and [even] in larger metropolitan communities" that do have access to alternatives and to specialized juvenile detention centers.[4]

Sarri also testified that existing studies indicate:

> [M]ost jails were more than fifty years old, dilapidated, and designed to service only the most dangerous offenders. Almost none have been constructed to permit humane segregation of juveniles from adults or of unsentenced from sentenced offenders. Sanitary conditions, food exercise facilities, fire control and so forth almost never met basic minimal public health requirements.[5]

She also told the subcommittee that despite the fact that the jailing of juveniles has been condemned by various national commissions, child advocacy groups, and child welfare reformers dating back to the turn of the century, the problem persists. She said: "Despite frequent and tragic stories of suicide, rape, and abuse of youth, the placement of juveniles in jail has not abated."[6] Sarri indicated that

she saw no reason to be optimistic about eliminating this problem
unless state laws were enacted that absolutely "prohibit the [deten-
tion and] commitment of juveniles to jail under any circumstances."[7]

In the winter of 1973, Senator Birch Bayh, chair of the subcommittee, introduced Senate Bill 821, the Juvenile Justice and Delinquency Prevention Act of 1973. The bill included a provision that
"juveniles alleged to be or found to be delinquent shall not be
detained or confined in any institutions in which adult persons
convicted of a crime or awaiting trial on criminal charges are
incarcerated."[8] The bill that ultimately was signed into law had been
watered down considerably. Unfortunately, one of the sections that
was altered was the section having to do with the jailing of juveniles.
The final version of the legislation was a compromise that essentially
allowed juveniles to be confined in jails so long as they were kept
separate from adult prisoners.

The jailing section was changed from Bayh's original proposal
because of concerns raised by Department of Justice officials from
the Federal Bureau of Prisons and the Law Enforcement Assistance
Administration, sheriffs, juvenile court judges, corrections professionals, and criminal justice planners. They were concerned about
the fact that there was an absence of community-based alternatives
and readily available secure detention facilities, particularly in rural
areas. These groups had the backing of some key Republican
senators, whose support was needed if a bill was to be passed that
had any chance of being signed by President Ford.

The compromise, though well-intentioned, turned out to be
disastrous. In many jurisdictions, juveniles incarcerated in jails
ended up being confined under worse conditions than adults. Jails
weren't built to house children. Consequently, in order to comply
with federal law and state statutes that may have been enacted to
comply with the federal mandate, sheriffs and jailers locked children
up in drunk tanks, segregation units, women's cell blocks, abandoned
sections of jails, and even makeshift cells in storage areas. Also,
because jails are almost always understaffed, the juveniles who were
confined received almost no supervision.

I've been an expert witness in dozens of lawsuits regarding the
conditions under which juveniles are incarcerated in jails, and I have
seen the results of the flawed policy firsthand. For example, the
Knox County, Kentucky, jail is more than 100 years old. The jail

fails to meet even the most minimal health, safety, fire, and program standards. Juveniles confined in the jail were placed either in the drunk tank or in one of two cells located in the back of the jail—in an area used to store cleaning equipment and voting machines. On the day I visited the facility in September 1982, I learned that two 14-year-old girls had recently been confined for ten days in one of the two cells in the storage area. The other cell had been occupied by a woman. During the night, adult male prisoners who were classified as trustees slept outside the cells on cots. The trustees provided some "supervision" at night, because no staff was on duty during the evening hours.

In August 1982, the federal court ruled that it was unconstitutional to house juveniles in adult jails in Oregon. The lawsuit that triggered that decision was initiated by the Oregon Legal Services Corporation and the National Center for Youth Law in St. Louis, Missouri, against the Columbia County jail in St. Helens, Oregon. The Columbia County jail was built in 1962 and remodeled in 1975. Juveniles who were incarcerated in the jail were kept in multiple-occupancy cells in a cell block usually reserved for women or in isolation rooms. There were instances in which several children between the ages of 12 and 17 were placed in the same cell. The isolation rooms had no windows, were made of concrete block, and had solid steel doors with peepholes. Each of the rooms had a sewer hole in the middle of the floor that the children had to use to urinate or defecate.

The jail staff had no special training in how to work with juveniles. Because the staff members were needed to supervise adult prisoners, particularly at night, the juveniles in the jail were left on their own. If they had a problem or needed to talk to a jail staff member, they had to scream or yell for assistance. Unlike adults, children confined in the jail didn't have access to books, television, radio, writing materials, or games. Also, although adult prisoners had regular visiting hours, the children did not.[9]

In 1979, the National Coalition for Jail Reform also recognized the disastrous implications of this policy. As a result, the coalition adopted the position that "no juvenile should be held in an adult jail"[10] and launched an aggressive campaign to inform and educate policymakers about the problem of incarcerating juveniles in jails. The coalition's publications, which were widely disseminated, noted that research conducted by the American Justice Institute indicated that "90 percent of the juveniles held in jails do not require secure detention."[11] The coalition was particularly effective in communicating the fact that juveniles in jail were high-risk candidates for suicide, physical and sexual abuse, and psychological trauma and that the potential for lawsuits was great.[12]

Jail Removal: A National Priority

The U.S. Department of Justice is not known for being on the cutting edge of social reform. However, I felt that it was essential that the department become more involved in juvenile justice policy issues and that the U.S. attorney general play an active role in the process. After all, the OJJDP was in the Department of Justice. Also, I was not unaware of the fact that when the attorney general spoke, people listened. I felt so strongly about this that I brought the subject up in the interview I had with Attorney General Benjamin Civiletti before I was nominated by President Carter to be the administrator of the OJJDP. To my pleasant surprise, I found Civiletti receptive and eager to be helpful.

The day-to-day management of the Department of Justice was delegated to Charles Renfrew, the deputy associate attorney general. I reported to Civiletti through Renfrew. Fortunately, I found Renfrew as receptive as Civiletti. More important, he was willing to spend some of his valuable time on juvenile justice issues. In fact, as it turned out, Renfrew ended up being the key player in the process. He was the person who needed to be convinced that removing juveniles from adult jails was the thing to do.

The National Coalition for Jail Reform had spent almost a year focusing national attention on the problem of juveniles in jails. They were definitely having an impact with their constituents and with state and local elected public officials. Accordingly, I asked one of my staff members, Doyle Wood, to take the lead role in developing an issue paper on jail removal that we could submit to the department for consideration. A couple of weeks after I sent the paper to the department for review, Jim Shine, my special assistant, and I met with Renfrew and his staff to discuss the issue and to recommend that removing juveniles from adult jails become departmental policy. Renfrew and his staff asked some tough questions. The tone of the meeting was supportive, however, and it appeared that Renfrew and his staff were favorably inclined toward the idea. The meeting ended with Renfrew agreeing to take the issue to Civiletti and recommend that he approve it.

On December 3, 1980, President Carter signed the reauthorization of the Juvenile Justice and Delinquency Prevention Act into law. The 1980 law contained the historic amendment regarding removal of juveniles from adult jails. Although it had been extremely difficult to find a member of Congress willing to sponsor the amendment, it had broad support and sailed through. Much of the congressional support that developed was garnered by Mark Davis, the OJJDP's congressional liaison, and Marion Mattingly, a citizen advocate from Maryland with a long-standing interest in juvenile justice and extraordinary political contacts. Davis and Mattingly visited congressional offices daily to make sure that the appropriate congressional staff members were informed on the issue—that they understood the importance of the legislation and were kept up-to-date on developments. Also, the members of the National Coalition for Jail Reform, particularly the National Association of Counties, played an extremely helpful role by involving their respective constituencies and by working the halls of Congress.

Opposition to the Jail Removal Amendment

Although the amendment breezed through Congress and was part of the legislation signed into law, it was not without opposition. The main source of opposition came from the National Criminal Justice Association (NCJA), a group that, ironically, was a member of the National Coalition for Jail Reform. The NCJA never came out publicly against the amendment to remove juveniles from adult jails, but they raised questions about it. Lee Thomas, president of the association and director of the Criminal Justice Planning Agency for South Carolina, served as the NCJA spokesman. Thomas testified on March 26, 1986, before the Subcommittee on the Constitution of the Committee on the Judiciary of the U.S. Senate. He questioned why juveniles must be removed from adult jails rather than simply kept from "having regular contact with adults." Thomas said that his association was interested in knowing:

1. what removal would accomplish that sight and sound separation would not;

2. whether removal of juveniles from adult jails would result in the building of more juvenile detention centers;

3. whether removing juveniles from adult jails would increase the number of juveniles waived to the adult court;

4. what progress had been made with respect to sight and sound separation;

5. how much it would cost to remove juveniles from adult jails; and

6. whether the five-year time requirement for removal would be adequate.[13]

The NCJA was made up of the state criminal justice planning agencies created by the now defunct federal Law Enforcement Assistance Administration (LEAA) program. The LEAA was created, in part, as a response to the recommendations of the 1967 President's Crime Commission. The state criminal justice planning agencies were set up to act as vehicles for the receipt and expenditure of federal crime control funds. With a few notable exceptions, these agencies allocated the overwhelming majority of these funds to the adult criminal justice system.[14] Much of the funding went into such things as armored cars, helicopters, radio and television equipment, and riot control gear.

The question of cost proved to be particularly significant. The reality was that there were no reliable figures regarding what it would cost to remove juveniles from adult jails. However, the experience in Pennsylvania, as well as in a few other jurisdictions, indicated that alternatives to jail (for example, twenty-four-hour on-call screening and crisis intervention services, family shelter care, home detention, professional staffed shelter care) were relatively inexpensive and could eliminate the incidence of jailing by 75 to 85 percent. Despite this, a number of states—with, I suspected, encouragement from NCJA—came up with grossly inflated estimates of what the price tag would be. For example, officials from Texas submitted an estimate to the House Rules Committee indicating that it would cost as much as a half-billion dollars to remove juveniles from jails in that state.[15] These inflated estimates were given for a variety of reasons. Officials in some states came up with ridiculous cost estimates because they wanted to show that removing juveniles from jail would be too expensive, so that Congress would back away from the issue. Some did it in the hope that Congress would allocate more funds to the juvenile justice program, particularly for the construction of detention centers.

Some of the state juvenile justice advisory committees were also opposed to the idea. These committees, created by the Juvenile Justice and Delinquency Prevention Act, were charged with the responsibility for comprehensive juvenile justice planning and for the administration of federal juvenile justice funds in their respective states. No one expected them to question the need to remove juveniles from adult jails, because they were supposed to be advocates for "enlightened" juvenile justice policies. Yet the leadership and staffs from a number of these committees raised questions similar to those raised by the NCJA.

The state juvenile justice advisory committees were upset and, to some extent, continue to be upset because they were not consulted on this issue and because it "was not initiated by states as an urgent item for the national agenda."[16] They are right on both counts.

There were a number reasons why they weren't consulted, particularly by me. Months before the Department of Justice decided to push for getting kids out of jails, I was on the road, speaking at juvenile justice and child welfare meetings all over the country. Wherever I went, I mentioned that the issue of removing juveniles from adult jails was under serious consideration by the OJJDP and the Department of Justice. My intent was both to alert people to the fact that the issue was being reviewed, and to test the waters by sampling some public reaction. Tom Parker, executive director of the NCJA, expressed to me privately that removing kids from jails was the right thing to do, but it was too controversial. He felt that local law enforcement officials, juvenile court judges, and probation workers wouldn't support it. Parker knew that local officials were putting some juveniles in jail for punishment and that they didn't want to have that option taken away from them. He was also concerned about the states that needed to build detention centers to house the youth who were accused of serious offenses. His feeling was that the amendment probably wouldn't get through Congress.

Concerns also filtered into the office from chairpersons and staff of state juvenile justice advisory committees all over the country. They complained that they were having enough trouble complying with the mandate to deinstitutionalize status offenders; they felt that having to get kids out of jails would only add to their problems. Some members of the state juvenile justice advisory committees were nervous that they would have to confront judges, probation and parole workers, and law enforcement officials in order to get them to stop throwing kids in jails. Jails were used in many jurisdictions because there were no other alternatives. However, judges and probation and parole staffs were locking many kids up in jails "to get their attention" or "to give them a taste" of what a harsh, prisonlike experience would be like.

I also avoided getting into direct discussion with the leadership of the state juvenile justice advisory groups because I had to work with a presidentially appointed national advisory committee to the OJJDP, and this committee was supposed to be the link with the state committees. Also, I was advised that the state juvenile justice advisory committees would eventually support the amendment because they wouldn't want to appear to be advocating against a progressive juvenile justice policy that had broad support. Moreover, the last thing I wanted to do was to be maneuvered into not moving on this issue until 51 percent of the chairpersons of the state juvenile justice advisory committees agreed that this was a good idea. It would have set a bad precedent and would have crippled the ability of the OJJDP to exercise leadership in the juvenile justice policy arena.

Our strategy for getting the amendment passed was to build so much support for it early in the process that any major organized opposition would be prevented from developing. We concentrated our efforts on such groups as the Association of Junior Leagues, the National Council of Jewish Women, the National Association of Counties, the PTA, organized labor, the Boys' and Girls' Clubs of America, and the YMCA and YWCA. These groups played a significant role in getting the act passed in 1974, and they were the juvenile justice program's bedrock of support. We also worked closely with and coordinated our efforts with the National Coalition for Jail Reform. I must admit that although I ignored the state juveniles justice committees at the time, some of them have proved to be key players in pushing for the removal of juveniles from jails in their respective jurisdictions.

The most unexpected and potentially troublesome source of opposition came from Mary Jolly, Senator Birch Bayh's key adviser on juvenile justice. Jolly's view was that the amendment "was redundant." She was of the opinion that the existing federal juvenile justice mandate to keep juveniles separate from adults in correctional facilities, if properly enforced, would essentially accomplish the same objective.[17]

Jolly called me on March 5, 1980, to say that a county attorney from Indiana (Senator Bayh's home state) wanted to talk to me about developing juvenile justice information systems for prosecuting attorneys. I took advantage of the opportunity to ask her about her concerns regarding the amendment, and our conversation became somewhat heated. As I recall, it ended with my telling her that I doubted that Senator Bayh would be against getting kids out of jail. Several days later, Mark Davis informed me that Jolly was "on board" with the amendment.

I doubt seriously that my telephone conversation with Jolly was responsible for her change of heart. She has good political instincts, and I suspect that she was moved when she learned which groups were behind the amendment and how strongly they felt. Besides, I can't imagine that she wanted to be responsible for putting Senator Bayh in the potentially embarrassing position of appearing not to support this important effort.

The Struggle Is Far from Over

Dr. Rosemary Sarri's testimony before Congress about the absence of comprehensive and reliable data regarding the numbers of juveniles in adult jails is almost as true today as when she delivered it in 1973. A few states have developed good jail systems, but most have not. The annual survey of inmates in local jails, administered by the Bureau of Justice Statistics, is considered the best and most reliable source of jail statistics. However, this data base has limitations. The survey does not include short-term lockups, state-administered jails, and the combined jail-prison systems in Connecticut, Delaware, Rhode Island, Hawaii, and Vermont.[18]

The best available evidence indicates that the number of juveniles admitted to adult jails nationally may be only just beginning to decline. An estimated 105,366 juveniles were admitted to adult jails in 1983. The number of admissions increased to 112,106 in 1985 and then declined to 92,856 in 1986.[19] However, as indicated in table 4–1, the one-day counts and rates of children in jails have not changed substantially since 1978, a full two years before the amendment calling for the removal of children from adult jails was incorporated into the Juvenile Justice and Delinquency Prevention Act. Moreover, the one-day counts increased to 1,708 in 1986, suggesting an upward trend since 1983.[20]

Although the national data are disappointing, these figures can be somewhat misleading. For example, there is considerable variation from state to state with respect to the incidence of juvenile jailing and the progress toward alleviating this problem. New York and Florida account for a disproportionate number of the juveniles confined in jails on any given day. For example, these two states accounted for 36 percent of all juveniles confined in adult jails on June 30, 1983. Also, New York and Florida reported a 400 percent increase in their one-day counts between 1978 and 1983. However, when New York and Florida's one-day counts of "[juvenile] jailing figures are removed from the [national] totals, there is actually a 26 percent decrease for the remaining states."[21]

The same appears to be the case with respect to the numbers of juveniles admitted annually to jails. Although the total annual admissions have not dropped substantially over the years, some states are reporting significant progress. For example, approximately 10,000 children were admitted to adult jails in Tennessee in 1982.

Table 4–1
JUVENILES IN ADULT JAILS
ONE-DAY COUNTS AND RATES, 1978 AND 1982–1984

Year	One-Day Counts	Rate per 100,000
1978	1,611	5.6
1982	1,729	6.3
1983	1,736	6.2
1984	1,482	5.6
1985	1,629	6.1

Source: Bureau of Justice Statistics, *Jail Inmates,* 1982, *Jail Inmates,* 1984, *Jail Inmates,* 1985. Washington, D.C.: U.S. Department of Justice.

Note: One-day counts are not available for 1979–81. Rate calculations are based on the numbers of juvenile betweens age 10 and the upper age of juvenile court jurisdiction in all fifty states and in the District of Columbia.

By 1984, the number had dropped to approximately 4,000. And in the first quarter of 1985, only 103 children were admitted to adult jails in that state.[22]

The number of juveniles admitted to adult jails in Colorado decreased from 6,117 in 1980 to 1,522 in 1984.[23] Officials in Michigan report that the number of juveniles admitted to adult jails in Michigan's Upper Peninsula, a predominately rural area, declined from 396 in 1980 to only 71 in 1985.[24]

Also, since 1984, legislation aimed at prohibiting the jailing of juveniles or restricting the number of admissions has been enacted in Illinois, Tennessee, Virginia, Missouri, North Carolina, and California.[25] In 1987, the Federal District Court for the Northern District of Iowa ruled that the jailing of juveniles in Iowa must come to an end.[26] More important, the court's decision essentially means that states that participate in the Juvenile Justice and Delinquency Prevention Act but are out of compliance with the act's mandates on juvenile jail removal can be sued.

Although it is clear that progress is being made toward eliminating juvenile jailing, the struggle is far from over. Juvenile admissions to adult jails continue to number in the tens of thousands each year, and most of the juveniles are confined for having been accused of committing relatively minor and petty crimes and status offenses. Also, there continues to be stiff resistance to ending this practice on the part of many judges, probation and parole workers, law enforcement officials, and state and local politicians. To be sure, a substantial number of juveniles are jailed because of a lack of alternatives. However, most are jailed for convenience, "to get their attention," or "to teach them a lesson."

For example, 3,720 juveniles were admitted to county jails and local lockups in Minnesota in 1985. As indicated in table 4–2, only 37 percent were admitted for Part I offenses. More than five times as many were confined for status offenses as for Part I violent crimes. The Minnesota jailing data also indicate that status offenders and juveniles accused of minor crimes were kept in jail as long as juveniles accused of serious property crimes. Also, as reflected in table 4–3, a substantially higher proportion of the juveniles accused of serious crimes against persons were released within six hours or less than was the case for those admitted for contempt of court, probation, and parole violations. This is an indicator of the irratio-

Table 4–2

JUVENILE ADMISSIONS TO JAILS AND LOCKUPS IN MINNESOTA, BY OFFENSE, 1985

Offenses	Number of Admissions	Percentage[a]
Part I violent crimes	123	3
Part I property crimes	1,265	34
Part II crimes	599	16
Status offenses	675	18
Public order offenses	363	10
Contempt of court	50	1
Probation/parole violation	340	9
Other	305	8
Totals	3720	100

Source: Minnesota Department of Corrections, 1986.

[a] Percentages may not total 100 because of rounding.

nality and depth of resistance to eliminating juvenile jailing on the part of many professionals who work in the system.

Another major problem is that virtually no attention has been focused on the number of juveniles housed in local police and sheriff's lockups. With the exception of a few states, there are no reliable data regarding the number of juveniles admitted to these facilities and, as yet, there has been no national and systematic attempt to gather such information. What little information exists suggests that the number of juveniles confined in these facilities may rival the number of juveniles incarcerated in adult jails.

For example, the California Youth Authority (CYA) reported that 99,709 juveniles were admitted to county jails and police lockups in that state in 1982.[27] The CYA then reported that the number of admissions had dropped to 11,249 in 1984 and to 9,995 in 1985.[28] At first glance, one might think that juvenile justice officials in California pulled off a minor miracle. However, "the drop-off of more than 88,000 jailings in two years was no miracle; it was simply a switch in the way the numbers are collected and reported."[29] Beginning in 1984, the CYA collected data only on juveniles admitted to jails and lockups who were held in excess of six hours. Because the overwhelming number of juveniles placed in such facilities, particularly lockups, are held for less than six hours, they are not reflected in the CYA figures.

Table 4–3

JUVENILES IN JAILS IN MINNESOTA, BY LENGTH OF STAY AND BY OFFENSE, 1985

	Length of Stay				
Offenses	Under 6 Hours	6–24 Hours	24 Hours to 8 Days	Over 8 Days	Totals
Part I	64	27	29	3	123
violent crimes	(52)	(22)	(24)	(2)	(100)
Part I	857	206	171	21	1255
property crimes	(68)	(16)	(14)	(2)	(100)
Part II	402	105	78	3	588
crimes	(68)	(18)	(13)	(1)	(100)
Status	464	147	50	1	662
offenses	(70)	(22)	(8)	(0)	(100)
Public	263	66	29	2	360
order offenses	(73)	(18)	(8)	(1)	(100)
Contempt	12	18	19	1	50
of court	(24)	(36)	(38)	(2)	(100)
Probation/	65	118	135	21	339
parole violations	(19)	(35)	(40)	(6)	(100)
Other	196	53	50	4	301
	(65)	(18)	(17)	(1)	(100)

Note: Percentages are given in parentheses. Percentages may not total 100 because of rounding.
Source: Minnesota Department of Corrections, 1986.

The statistics tell only part of the story. They say nothing about the abuses in these facilities. For example, it was reported in April 1986 that 6-year-old Daniel Bartsh was "arrested and booked in jail [in Winter Springs, Florida] for pocketing a 35-cent packet of bubble gum at a convenience store." Bartsh was so shaken by the experience that he refused to go to school the next day "without taking a security blanket with him."[30]

In August 1986, private attorneys in Portland, Maine—with assistance from the Youth Law Center in San Francisco—filed a class action lawsuit against the jail in Cumberland County. The suit alleged that Eric, a 13-year-old boy, was incarcerated in the jail for stealing a dirtbike. He was confined next to a 17-year-old who was being held for assault and who had a history of violent and sexual offenses. The suit indicated that the staff left the cell doors open and that the 17-year-old sexually assaulted Eric and forced him to have oral intercourse with him.[31]

The bill that essentially eliminates the jailing of juveniles in

California was signed by Governor Deukmejian in 1986. However, Clancy Leland, legislative representative for Los Angeles County, sent a letter to the bill's author in the legislature, stating that the Los Angeles County Board of Supervisors opposed the bill. He wrote: "There is a perceived national problem of children inappropriately held in adult jails. The existence of such a problem has not been clearly demonstrated in California."[32] Evidently, Leland and the members of the Los Angeles County Board were unaware of or indifferent to the following facts:

- In 1983, "for example, Kathy Sue Robbins, a 15-year-old, was locked in the Glenn County Jail in California for running away from home. Four days later she committed suicide by hanging herself from a bunk rail."[33]
- There were 1,651 children confined in the Long Beach City Jail between January 1, 1985, and April 30, 1985. Of the juveniles incarcerated, 317 were status offenders and 318 were dependent, neglected, and abused children. Between January 1, 1985, and May 21, 1985, at least 54 dependent children were incarcerated for more than six hours in the jail.[34]

Discussion

The juvenile justice system is beleaguered by problems, but none is more pressing than the issue of the jailing of children. Although there is evidence that some progress is being made in this area— particularly since the 1980 amendment to the Juvenile Justice and Delinquency Prevention Act, calling for the removal of juveniles from adult jails, was enacted—the problem persists. We must make every effort to keep this issue at the top of the juvenile justice reform agenda and to bring this shameful practice to an end as quickly as possible.

It is particularly important that strategies be implemented to inform and educate state and local elected officials, law enforcement personnel, and judges about the hazards and liabilities of jailing children. Jails lack adequate physical plant facilities, adequate numbers of appropriately trained staff members, as well as adequate health, recreational, and other programs to meet the minimum standards of juvenile confinement. These problems, coupled with the potential risks of suicide and other forms of abuse, put jails at great risk of litigation. Counties and municipalities that operate jails that confine children do not generally have liability insurance to cover the costs of such litigation. Also, sheriffs are increasingly being held accountable for what happens in their jails, and punitive damages are being awarded from their personal assets.

It is essential that state and local elected public officials, as well as others, be made aware of the fact that alternatives to the use of jails are relatively inexpensive and can be implemented without sacrificing public safety. Such alternatives as twenty-four-hour on-call screening and crisis intervention services, family shelter care, and staff-operated shelter care could handle 80 percent or more of the juveniles being jailed each year. For those few who need secure custody confinement pending their appearance in court, a small number of strategically located secure beds or temporary holding facilities could be developed pending their transfer to a detention facility. For example, it is estimated that between six and eight strategically located secure detention beds are needed to remove children from adult jails and local lockups in Minnesota.

As I mentioned earlier, I wanted to take advantage of the opportunity of serving as the administrator of the Office of Juvenile Justice and Delinquency Prevention to launch a campaign aimed at removing children from adult jails and police lockups. I knew that the only way to launch a sustained effort was to make it a statutory mandate of the Juvenile Justice Act. I knew at the time that the requirement that states comply with the new mandate within a five-year period would most likely be extended. However, my real goal was to see juveniles removed from adult jails and lockups by the end of the decade.

The Carter administration was genuinely committed to this initiative. At a time when federal agencies were told to hold the line on expenditures, the Department of Justice recommended a substantial increase (34 percent) in the fiscal year 1981–82 budget for the OJJDP. The increase was largely to be targeted at juvenile jail removal.

When the Reagan administration took over, they immediately

proceeded to try to kill the federal juvenile justice program altogether. Fortunately, the program was kept alive by Congress, although at a significantly reduced funding level. The cuts in funding obviously had an adverse impact on the entire federal juvenile justice program. What is particularly tragic is that the cuts stymied progress on removing children from adult penal facilities. Even more tragic was that Reagan administration officials were indifferent to this problem. They claimed that the goal of removing children from adult jails had largely been accomplished—and that it was a state and local problem anyway. It is interesting that the Reagan administration felt that the problem of serious juvenile crime was an appropriate issue for the federal government to be concerned about. Juvenile crime, whether serious or not, is also a state and local problem. I fail to see any significant differences that would justify elevating serious juvenile crime to the federal domestic policy agenda but not removal of children from adult jails, except that serious juvenile crime happened to be more politically popular at the time.

Despite these difficulties, some progress has been made on this issue. In some states and local jurisdictions, juvenile jailing has been either eliminated or substantially curtailed. Moreover, it is doubtful that there would have been any major state legislative advances in this area without the 1980 juvenile jail removal amendment to the federal act.

We must not lose sight of the fact that the confinement of juveniles in adult jails and police lockups is still one of the most serious problems confronting the juvenile justice system. We must also face the fact that there probably will not be any major progress on this issue until legislation is enacted in every state that prohibits the incarceration of juveniles in adult institutions.

Notes

1. The National Coalition for Jail Reform was dedicated to improving the conditions in our nation's jails and preventing the incarceration of certain groups of people (for example, the mentally ill, the mentally retarded, and the public inebriant). The coalition's members included such groups as the American Bar Association, the American Civil Liberties Union, the American

Correctional Association, the American Correctional Health Services Association, the American Friends Service Committee, the American Jail Association, the American Public Health Association, the Benedict Center for Criminal Justice, the John Howard Association, the National Association of Blacks in Criminal Justice, the National Association of Counties, the National Association of Trial Court Administrators, the National Center for State Courts, the National Council on Crime and Delinquency, the National Criminal Justice Association, the National Institute of Corrections, the National Inter-Religious Task Force on Criminal Justice, the National League of Cities, the National Legal Aid and Defender Association, the National Sheriff's Association, the National Urban League, the Police Executive Research Forum, the Southern Coalition on Jails and Prisons, and the United States Conference of Mayors.

2. U.S. Congress, House (1980), p. 38.
3. U.S. Congress, Senate (1973a), p. 23.
4. Ibid.
5. Ibid., p. 26.
6. Ibid., p. 23.
7. Ibid., p. 34.
8. U.S. Congress, Senate (1973b), p. 343.
9. *D.B. v. Tewksburg* (1982), pp. 896–905.
10. National Coalition for Jail Reform (1985), p. 11.
11. National Coalition for Jail Reform (undated), p. 2.
12. Ibid., pp. 1–2.
13. U.S. Congress, Senate (1980), p 466.
14. U.S. Congress, Senate (1973a), p. 182.
15. Raley (1982), pp. 8–9.
16. National Coalition of State Juvenile Justice Advisory Groups (1986), p. 29.
17. National Council on Crime and Delinquency (1980), p. 5.
18. U.S. Department of Justice (1987), p. 5.
19. Ibid., p. 2.
20. Ibid.
21. Community Research Associates (updated = a), p. 2.
22. American Bar Association (undated), p. 3.
23. Martinez (1986).
24. Community Research Associates (undated = b), p. 8.
25. Steinhart and Krisberg (1987) p. 13.
26. *Hendrickson v. Griggs* (1987).
27. Department of Youth Authority (1983), p. i.
28. Department of Youth Authority (1986), p. i.
29. Private Sector Task Force on Juvenile Justice (1985), p. 3.
30. *Gainesville Sun* (1986).
31. *Eric P v. Cumberland County, Maine* (1984), p. 14.
32. Leland (1986), p. 3.
33. Steinhart (1986), pp. 1–2.
34. *Baumgartner v. City of Long Beach* (1985), pp. 3–5.

References

American Bar Association, Juvenile Justice Committee, Criminal Justice Section. Undated. *Information Packet on Juveniles in Adult Jails.* Washington, D.C.: American Bar Association.

Community Research Associates. Undated = a. *Jail Removal in the States: Where Do We Stand?* Champaign, Ill.: Community Research Associates.

————. Undated = b. *The Michigan Holdover Network: Short Term Supervision Stategies for Rural Counties.* Champaign, Ill.: Community Research Associates.

Department of Youth Authority, State of California. 1983. *The 1982 Jail Report: Minors Detained in California Jails and Lockups in 1982.* Sacramento: California Youth Authority.

————. 1986. *The 1985 Jail Report: Minors Detained in California Jails and Lockups in 1985.* Sacramento: California Youth Authority.

Gainesville (Fla.) Sun. 6 April 1986. "Six-year-old is charged with theft of bubble-gum."

Leland, C., Legislative Representative, Los Angeles County Board of Supervisors. 7 August 1986. Letter to State Senator Robert Presley.

Martinez, O. 9 December 1986. Letter to author.

National Coalition for Jail Reform. Undated. *Juveniles and Jails: The Wrong Combination—A Resource Packet.* Washington, D.C.: National Coalition for Jail Reform.

————. 1985. *A Unique Experiment.* Washington, D.C.: National Coalition for Jail Reform.

National Coalition of State Juvenile Justice Advisory Groups. 1986. *The First Report to the President, the Congress and the Administrator of the Office of Juvenile Justice and Delinquency Prevention.* n.pl.: National Coalition of State Juvenile Justice Advisory Groups.

National Council on Crime and Delinquency. 1980. "Removal of All Youths from Jails Proposed." *Criminal Justice Newsletter* 11 (7): 5.

Private Sector Task Force on Juvenile Justice. 1985. *Children in California Jails.* San Francisco: National Council on Crime and Delinquency.

Raley, G. 1982. "Removing Children from Adult Jails: The Dance of Legislation." *Children's Legal Rights Journal* 3 (6): 4–9.

Steinhart, D. 9 September 1986. Memo to All Interested Parties.

Steinhart, D., and Krisberg, B. 1987. "Children in Jail." *State Legislatures* 13 (3): 12–16.

U.S. Congress, House, Committee on Education and Labor, Subcommittee on Human Resources. 1980. *Juvenile Justice Amendments of 1980.* 96th Cong., 2d sess.

U.S. Congress, Senate, Committee on the Judiciary, Subcommittee to Investigate Juvenile Delinquency. 1973a. *The Detention and Jailing of Juveniles.* 93d Cong., 1st sess.

————. 1973b. *The Juvenile Justice and Delinquency Prevention Act—S.3148 and S.821.* 92d Cong., 2d sess.; 93d Cong., 1st sess.

————. 1980. *Reauthorization of the Juvenile Justice and Delinquency Prevention Act of 1974.* 96th Cong., 2 sess.

U.S. Department of Justice, Bureau of Justice Statistics. 1987. *Jail Inmates 1986*. Washington, D.C.: U.S. Government Printing Office.

Legal Cases

Baumgartner v. City of Long Beach. Civ. No. C-54782, Memorandum of Points and Authorities in Support of Plaintiff's Motion for a Preliminary Injunction. Superior Court of the State of California for the County of Los Angeles (1985).
D.B. v. Tewskbury, 545 F. Supp. (D. Oregon 1982).
Hendrickson v. Griggs. 672 F. Supp. 1126 (N.D. Iowa 1987).
Eric P v. Cumberland County, Maine. Civil Rights Complaint for Declaratory, Injunctive, and Other Equitable Relief and Damages (Class Action) and Demand for Jury Trial. U.S. District Court for the District of Maine (1986).

5

The Child Advocates

C HILD advocacy organizations, public interest groups, professional associations, national youth-serving agencies, elected
public officials, and reformers were instrumental in mobilizing
support for the enactment of the Juvenile Justice and Delinquency
Prevention Act of 1974. Many of these groups and individuals were
genuinely concerned about the plight of children and were not afraid
to advocate for what they felt was right. They were also politically
astute. Their years of experience in children and youth issues at the
local, state, and national levels made them wise in the ways of
politics and in how to get things done.

However, not all of the groups that advocated for and supported
the act turned out to be primarily interested in juvenile justice
reform or even in the best interests of children. Some of them—
particularly groups that received large amounts of federal juvenile
justice funds—became so dependent on federal funds that they
became far more concerned with advocating for themselves and
keeping the federal monies flowing into their coffers than with
children.

Two representatives of the National Youth Workers Alliance
(NYWA) stopped by to see me in March 1980. I was looking forward
to the meeting, because the NYWA was the largest consortium of
youth worker and child advocacy organizations in the country. Also,
the NYWA was politically active and influential on youth issues (for
example, youth employment, child welfare, juvenile justice, children's health care) at the federal and state levels.

I assumed that the NYWA would be active in the reauthorization
of the Juvenile Justice and Delinquency Prevention Act. I wanted to

talk with them about the Department of Justice's interest in the amendment calling for the removal of juveniles from adult jails, and I wanted to enlist NYWA support on this issue. I also wanted to discuss another proposed amendment to the act, one strongly backed by the National Council of Juvenile and Family Court Judges. It was an amendment that would allow status offenders to be locked up and essentially treated like delinquents if they violated a court order (for example, refused to go to school, ran away from home, disobeyed their parents, ran away from a placement).

I asked my assistant, Jim Shine, to sit in on the meeting. We started off with coffee and small talk. We discussed youth-related activities in the Departments of Labor and Health and Human Services and talked specifically about some of the youth employment and education issues that the NYWA was concerned about. They told me that the NYWA was putting on a national annual youth workers conference in Washington, D.C., and they asked if I'd be willing to speak at the meeting. I sensed a bit of tension in the air but paid no attention to it.

The small talk came to an abrupt end when one of the NYWA representatives said to me, "If you don't give NYWA a half-million dollars, we won't support the reauthorization of the J.J. Act." I thought he was joking, although I couldn't tell for sure. He advised that I remember who the "real friends" of the Juvenile Justice and Delinquency Prevention Act were and who my friends were. He said that those were the groups I should be giving discretionary grants to. He said the NYWA had been "cut out of the action" ever since my predecessor, John Rector, had left office.

I turned to the other person from NYWA and asked him if his associate was serious. He replied that he was "dead serious." I looked at Shine. The expression on his face indicated that he had no idea what was going on.

I didn't know what to say. I had never been in such a situation before, although I wasn't naive and I knew that influential groups threw their weight around in Washington all the time. I also knew that that's how some of them extracted big bucks from the federal government. After collecting my thoughts, I told them that if NYWA support for the reauthorization was contingent on my giving them money, we would get the act reauthorized without NYWA support. I also said that I was going to assume that they had had a bad day and suggested that they call me in a couple of weeks so that we could start over.

They did call me back, and I met with representatives of the NYWA on a number of occasions. As it turned out, the NYWA played an active and important role in the 1980 reauthorization process. However, the experience sensitized me to realities of the politics of juvenile justice.

With Friends Like These, Who Needs Enemies?

Jerry Miller, former commissioner of the Department of Youth Services in Massachusetts, describes the history of juvenile justice as one characterized by cycles of reform and retrenchment. Miller maintains that scandals, particularly those that occur in the institutions, are followed by public outcry. This leads to reforms, followed by periods of stability and indifference. Then the cycle is repeated. The casualties in this process usually end up being the bureaucrats who manage the system, particularly the heads of youth corrections agencies, institutional superintendents, chief probation officers, and the like. Rarely are the real powerbrokers called to account, especially those who so self-righteously claim to be acting in the "best interests" of children.

The National Council of Juvenile and Family Court Judges

One of the most significant sources of power and influence over the lives of children and the formulation of youth policy in practically every community is the juvenile court. Historically, juvenile court judges have played an important role in improving the quality of justice for children and in advocating for needed services. They helped lead the fight to remove juveniles from adult prisons at the turn of the century. They were instrumental in the development of probation services, group homes, and halfway houses for delinquent youth, and they have been forceful advocates of services for dependent, neglected, and abused children.

In 1937, a group of concerned juvenile court judges founded the National Council of Juvenile and Family Court Judges. The council is "dedicated to improving the juvenile justice system" in the United States.[1] Its purposes are

- To improve standards and effectiveness in the nation's juvenile and family courts.
- To conduct training and educational programs for persons in the field of juvenile justice.
- To provide technical assistance and information to courts and agencies concerned with children.
- To conduct research and disseminate findings for practical use by those in the field.
- To publish periodicals and educational materials for use of those in the field, allied professionals, and the general public.[2]

Over the years, the council has established itself as an influential and respected organization. Its advice has been sought by national and state legislative bodies, presidential commissions, national standards-setting groups, professional associations, and public interest groups. It was instrumental in mobilizing support for the enactment of the Juvenile Justice and Delinquency Prevention Act of 1974. According to former senator Birch Bayh, chief architect of the act: "The juvenile court judges knew how to pick up the phone and talk to their senator or congressman." In recent years, the council's reputation has slipped. I think it has slipped because the council has become dependent upon and corrupted by the availability of federal funds and has lost sight of its mission.

Fearing the loss of federal support for its research and training programs because of the Reagan administration's proposal to "zero out" the budget of the OJJDP, Arne Schoeller, the council's director of planning and development, sent a memo to the council's officers and trustees. The memo, dated February 20, 1981, alerted them to the implications of what the loss of federal funds would mean to the council's programs. In the memo, Schoeller indicated that the council has "been the severest critic" of how the federal juvenile justice program has been administered and is "the most conservatively perceived" of the Juvenile Justice and Delinquency Prevention Act supporters. This, he maintained, meant that the council was "well positioned to argue in the Congress and through the Congress to the administration that a separate juvenile delinquency program *should* be maintained" but with substantially "revised priorities."[3] The implication was that the philosophy of the National Council of Juvenile and Family Court Judges was in tune with the ideology of the incoming Reagan administration.

Apparently, what was meant by suggesting that a change of program priorities was needed was, in part, that the council should advocate for keeping certain individuals and groups whose ideas or philosophy differed from the council's from receiving federal juvenile justice funds. When it became evident that the federal juvenile justice program was going to survive, Schoeller wrote another memo. This memo, dated October 26, 1982, was addressed to two of the council's more active and influential members. Schoeller wrote that the OJJDP was planning to give out some grants for the training of juvenile justice personnel. He stated that the staff of the office knew "very little about training" and that "they have some *very misguided ideas* [and] are inclined to recommend exactly the *wrong* people or outfits to give the money to, or for faculty, etc."[4]

The list of undesirables in Schoeller's memo included Ted Rubin, former juvenile court judge from Denver, Colorado, and director of the highly regarded Institute for Court Management; Barbara Flicker and David Gilman, former staff members of the Institute for Judicial Administration/American Bar Association Project on Juvenile Justice Standards; Harry Swanger, former director of the National Center for Youth Law, St. Louis, Missouri; the National Youth Workers Alliance; and the National Legal Aid and Defenders Association (NLADA).

Ted Rubin was known for his enlightened policies when he served on the juvenile court bench in Denver. As a judge, he advocated for and relied heavily on community-based alternatives and used incarceration very sparingly. Rubin's philosophy conflicted with that of a number of the juvenile court judges who controlled the council. David Gilman and Barbara Flicker were the key staff members of the Institute for Judicial Administration/American Bar Association Project on Juvenile Justice Standards, which produced the most widely used and generally accepted standards in the field—standards vigorously opposed by the National Council of Juvenile and Family Court Judges.

Harry Swanger, a prominent public interest attorney and former director of the National Center for Youth Law in St. Louis, has successfully litigated cases involving children who have been abused in institutions, particularly in training schools and adult jails. His suits have often resulted in a ban on the jailing of children and curtailed use of training schools, practices that many judges support. The National Youth Workers Alliance (NYWA) and its state and local affiliates fought hard, but unsuccessfully, to try to kill the "valid court order" amendment that was tacked on to the Juvenile Justice Act when it was reauthorized in 1980. The "valid court order" amendment was the brainchild of the National Council of Juvenile and Family Court Judges. It was a measure designed to allow the courts to incarcerate runaways and school truants who disobey a court order and handle them like juvenile criminals or delinquents. The NYWA and its affiliates also supported diverting as many children as possible from the juvenile court system. This was another concept that was less than enthusiastically endorsed by the council, because it could have meant that upwards of 40 percent of the cases appearing before the juvenile courts in some jurisdictions would be eliminated from the courts' caseload. This would have raised a lot of questions about the resources being pumped into the juvenile courts and about whether they could be better utilized elsewhere. Diverting status offenders from the juvenile justice system meant that the courts would essentially be out of the business of ordering children to attend school, to stop running away from home, and to obey their parents, under the threat of incarceration— a practice that never worked anyway. With respect to the NLADA, the concern was that any grant to this group would "turn out to be another form of 'advocacy to attack the system,' especially juvenile judges."[5]

One of the two judges to whom Schoeller's memo was addressed was Judge John R. Milligan of Ohio. Judge Milligan, who now serves on the Ohio Court of Appeals for the 5th District, forwarded Schoeller's memo to Bud Wilkinson, along with a cover memo he wrote himself. Wilkinson, a television sportscaster and once head football coach at the University of Oklahoma, was President Reagan's appointee to chair the National Advisory Committee to the OJJDP.

Judge Milligan was hoping to get the advisory committee to look into this matter and do something about it. He wrote:

The enclosed deserves our attention. If the bureaucracy executes grants for training to NYWA and Ted Rubin . . . the thinking of most of us continues to be frustrated by the anti-system people.

Flicker and NLADA are no better.

Do we want to stop this—and if so, how?[6]

In 1981, the National Council of Juvenile and Family Court Judges issued a publication entitled *Bench Sense*, which was a critical review of the implementation of the Juvenile Justice and Delinquency Prevention Act. The document contained some good ideas and recommendations for improving the program, but it was also riddled with inaccuracies and distortions that detracted from its utility and added to the credibility problems of the organization. For example, *Bench Sense* noted that the council supported the removal of juveniles from adult jails. However, the publication implied that most of the juveniles who were confined in adult jails were there for having committed serious crimes.[7] The truth is that the overwhelming majority of children who are jailed every year are status offenders, probation and parole violators, and juveniles accused of committing minor and petty offenses. It would be awkward for the National Council of Juvenile and Family Court Judges to proclaim publicly that they were in favor of jailing children. After all, juvenile court judges are supposed to be concerned with the "best interests" of children. However, since many of the council's members, particularly some of its more active members, support the practice and send kids to jail regularly, a distorted picture was presented in an effort to try to slow down and, if possible, block progress on this critically important issue.

The report also noted that when I was the administrator of the OJJDP, I failed to inform "the Congress [about] the results of the national evaluation of the deinstitutionalization of status offenders' programs [during the reauthorization hearings], although they were available in preliminary form in 1980." The report implied that I withheld the report because the findings did "not support OJJDP's position on deinstitutionalization."[8] This, too, was inaccurate. At the time of the 1980 reauthorization hearings before the House Subcommittee on Human Resources, the full study had not yet been submitted and the executive summary was in draft form. The policy of the Office of Juvenile Justice was not to release research and program evaluation findings until they were in final form. Moreover, and contrary to the implications in *Bench Sense*, the results indicated "that the secure confinement of status offenders provides no gain in deterrence over provision of community services."[9]

What is particularly revealing about this episode is the fact that the National Council of Juvenile and Family Court Judges had copies of the preliminary report long before *Bench Sense* was published and before the reauthorization of the Juvenile Justice and Delinquency Prevention Act was finalized. I made an exception to the general policy of the office and sent copies to the national council's president, government committee chairman, and executive director. I did this to refute their accusations that my staff and I were trying to conceal a report that would be damaging to the act's mandate calling for the removal of status offenders from secure facilities (detention centers, training schools, and adult jails)—a mandate that, as mentioned earlier, many of the council's membership didn't agree with.

Judge Milligan wrote to the chair of the House Subcommittee on Human Resources, the oversight committee for juvenile justice in the House, and essentially leveled some of the same charges that appeared later in *Bench Sense*. Gordon A. Raley, the staff director to the subcommitte, sent a reply to Milligan on behalf of the chair. Raley indicated that he, too, was "curious about why the office did not make [the report] . . . available to the subcommittee prior to [the] hearings."[10] However, Raley's curiosity was aroused not because he thought the office was "intentionally trying to withhold information, but because the information seems so supportive" of the federal legislative policies mandating the deinstitutionalization of status offenders.[11]

Another, albeit more subtle, activity of the council that raises eyebrows in the legal community and among many judges who are not affiliated with the organization has to do with the national training conferences of the council. These conferences are designed for juvenile justice professionals, educators, state and local elected public officials, child health and mental health professionals, and other groups interested in children's issues. Curiously, the council primarily cosponsors these meetings with only one other national group—the National District Attorney's Association. This "cooperative" relationship between these two groups gives the appearance that the juvenile court judges are "in bed" with the prosecutors. It further undermines the credibility of the national council and, more important, raises serious questions about the independence and objectivity of the juvenile court as an institution.

The political wheeling and dealing of the National Council of Juvenile and Family Court Judges has paid off. The council received a $1.5 million pledge from the U.S. Department of Justice to build a new continuing judicial education center at the University of Nevada—Reno.[12] Also, the council's budget ballooned from $2.48 million in fiscal year 1982–83 to more than $5.3 million in fiscal year 1984–85, with more than 61 percent of those revenues coming from federal and state sources.[13]

Fortunately, the National Council of Juvenile and Family Court Judges is not representative of the broader judicial community. For example, the Conference of Chief Justices recently adopted a strongly worded resolution calling for elimination of the jailing of juveniles and urging state policymakers and professionals to take steps to bring an end to this practice as quickly as possible.[14] In referring to this resolution, Chief Justice Robert Murphy of Maryland, president of the Conference of Chief Justices, remarked that he thought "it should be obvious to everyone that an adult jail is no place for a child."[15]

State Juvenile Justice Advisory Committees

The Juvenile Justice and Delinquency Prevention Act of 1974 required that states choosing to participate in the federal juvenile justice program have a juvenile justice advisory committee appointed by their governors. It was hoped that these committees would play a leadership role in state juvenile justice planning and policy development, would serve as catalysts and advocates for change, and would oversee the administration of federal juvenile justice funds. It was assumed that because the members would be appointed by the governor, they would have access to each state's key elected public officials, juvenile justice professionals, human service administrators, and opinion leaders.

The advisory committees in some states have had and are continuing to have a significant impact. Pennyslvania's advisory committee provided leadership in helping to remove juveniles from adult jails in that state several years before Congress made it a national priority. The committee in Massachusetts has been a key actor in the development of juvenile justice policy and plays an important role in that state's internationally recognized juvenile corrections system.

Unfortunately, these examples are the exception rather than the rule. Most state juvenile justice advisory committees do little or no comprehensive planning. Even if they did, hardly anyone would pay any attention to them, because they tend to have little or no clout. They are usually buried in some state agency and exist primarily to capture the small amount of federal monies to which the state is entitled.

In Georgia, at a recent statewide governor's conference on juvenile justice, Justice Thomas O. Marshall, chief justice of the state's supreme court, remarked: "Georgia needs a visible, central state-wide body for juvenile justice policy planning to build consensus and to establish, monitor, and measure system goals."[16] Marshall observed that the existing state juvenile justice advisory committee "is not as visible as Georgia's planning body must be [and that] . . . in some ways it is now structured to be ignored."[17] Marshall could just as well have been describing the advisory committees in most other states.

The impotence of some of these groups can also be seen by developments surrounding legislation that was recently passed in California to remove juveniles from adult jails. The proposed legislation was supported by the California Police Officers Association; the California Sheriffs Association; the California Chiefs of Police Association; the California Probation, Parole and Correctional Association; the attorney general of California; the Juvenile Justice Section of the California State Bar; the Juvenile Justice Committee of the Los Angeles County Bar Association; the National Council on Crime and Delinquency; the California Parent–Teachers Association; and the American Civil Liberties Union. Noticeably absent from the list was the California Juvenile Justice Advisory Committee.[18] When I inquired about this, the juvenile justice specialist for the California committee told me that the group did not play a role in the jail removal legislation because the committee "does not take positions on issues of juvenile justice policy." He said the advisory committee discussed the bill "only to a minor extent" and that the committee "could not take a position on it until the governor's position was known."

What is even more troubling is the fact that the juvenile justice advisory committees in a number of states have remained silent or have chosen to ignore abusive and unprofessional practices. The advisory committees in such states as Oregon, Colorado, Arizona, Washington, California, Florida, Alabama, Tennessee, Louisiana, Kentucky, New Hampshire, West Virginia, Idaho, Maine, Maryland, Ohio, and the District of Columbia have been remarkably quiet while children have been abused and mistreated in adult jails, detention centers, or training schools in their jurisdictions. In some instances, committee members have been reluctant to associate with or have been downright hostile to private attorneys and public interest lawyers who have filed lawsuits to end these abuses. Some of the lawsuits have been against training schools administered by state executive branch agencies. Because these institutions are usually managed by someone appointed by a governor and because the governor is usually named as a defendant in the suit, juvenile justice advisory committee members have tended to keep quiet about the merits of the litigation in fear of falling into disfavor with the person who appointed them to the committee.

I recall attending a state juvenile justice advisory committee meeting in Idaho. I was accompanied by a lawyer from the Youth Law Center in San Francisco, the group that brought suit against the training school in St. Anthony, Idaho. As we entered the building where the meeting was scheduled to take place, we bumped into one of the advisory committee members. She told us she was glad that the problems at the training school were finally being dealt with. She also asked us to wait a few minutes before going into the meeting because she didn't think it would "look too good" for her to be seen walking into the room with us.

People and Events That Have Made a Difference

The *Gault* decision is, by far, the single most important event in the history of juvenile justice. Since that 1967 decision, a number of other noteworthy events and individuals have made important contributions to the field.

The inquiry into the juvenile justice system during the late 1960s and early 1970s by the U.S. Senate Subcommittee to Investigate Juvenile Delinquency was the most comprehensive and in-depth

examination of the juvenile justice system that has ever been
undertaken. The pioneering work of that body and the extraordinary
leadership of its chair, Senator Birch Bayh, led to the enactment of
the landmark Juvenile Justice and Delinquency Prevention Act of
1974. The subcommittee performed an invaluable service by opening
up the innards of the juvenile justice system to public scrutiny, and
it built the bipartisan congressional support needed to make juvenile
justice a national priority.

The 1980 amendment to the act, calling for the removal of
juveniles from adult jails and police lockups, will undoubtedly be
remembered as one of the most important advances in juvenile
justice and child welfare. Also, when the history of juvenile justice
reform is written, former Colorado congressman Ray Kogovsek will
be remembered for the courage and leadership he exhibited in
helping to make this a reality.

In 1972, Jerry Miller, then commissioner of the Department of
Youth Services in Massachusetts, and his assistants closed down all
of that state's large juvenile training schools. It was an event that sent
shock waves through the entire American juvenile justice and child
welfare establishment. Miller was branded a lunatic and was severely
criticized by juvenile justice and child welfare professionals and
organizations throughout the country. To be sure, when the training
schools were first closed, there was chaos and uncertainty. Alternative programs for handling the youth who had been housed in the
training schools either were in short supply or didn't exist. Now,
more than fifteen years later, few would argue with the fact that
Massachusetts' scandal-ridden training schools needed to be closed
and that Miller did the right thing. Moreover, a ten-year evaluation
of the Massachusetts experience by researchers from the Harvard
Center for Criminal Justice concluded that it was a success and that,
if anything, Miller and his colleagues didn't go far enough in
implementing the reform measures.[19]

Today, policymakers and administrative officials in nearly half the
states are in the process of reexamining their juvenile crime control
policies. Many of these states are considering reforms similar to
those implemented in Massachusetts. Miller is anything but a
lunatic. A more accurate description, in my opinion, comes from
Scott Matheson, former Utah governor, who refers to Miller as "a
thoughtful and caring person with sensible ideas." When the full

history of juvenile justice in America is written, I suspect that Miller will emerge as one of the key actors in the latter half of this century.

The lawyers—both public interest and private—who represent children who are abused in institutions or who have had their constitutional rights violated are also making a difference. These are some of the "anti-system people" the National Council of Juvenile and Family Court Judges are so concerned about. This is understandable, because these lawyers attack practices condoned by many judges. They also attack abusive practices in detention centers, institutions often administered by the juvenile courts. The detention center in Cleveland, Ohio, is a case in point. It is also illustrative of some of the interesting interconnections in the world of the juvenile court. The detention center is under the administrative control of the courts. Judge John Toner, once a member of the board of trustees of the National Council of Juvenile and Family Court Judges, was the presiding judge of the juvenile court in Cleveland during the time that institution was successfully sued for abusive practices, unconstitutional conditions of confinement, and violations of civil rights.[20] Walter G. Whitlach, now the "historian" of the council, retired from the juvenile bench in Cleveland shortly before the litigation got under way.

Although legal aid and public interest lawyers are both feared and despised by many judges, elected public officials, and youth corrections professionals, many of the states whose youth detention and corrections systems have been under litigation, or have felt the threat of litigation, have stopped abusing children and/or have experienced dramatic declines in the number of juveniles incarcerated. As indicated in table 5–1, there has been almost a 60 percent decline in the rate of commitments to training schools between 1979 and 1984 in five states where there has been some type of litigation. This compares with only a 2 percent reduction in the rate of commitments for all the other states and the District of Columbia combined during the same period.

In Colorado, the threat of litigation precipitated a study of the state's youth corrections system by the National Council on Crime and Delinquency. This led to the enactment of the legislative reform package referred to in chapter 3, which promises that the state will have a vastly improved youth corrections system with substantially fewer institutional beds than now exist. Where suits have been filed

Table 5–1

COMMITMENTS TO TRAINING SCHOOLS IN
SELECTED STATES WHERE LITIGATION HAS
OCCURRED, 1979 AND 1984

State	1979		1984		
	Number	Rate per 100,000	Number	Rate per 100,000	Percentage Change in Rate
Louisiana	1,467	271	828	144	−47
Florida	2,747	241	923	80	−67
Idaho	231	178	122	90	−49
Oklahoma	598	158	215	55	−65
Utah	391	193	180	77	−60
Totals	5,434	227	2268	91	−60

Source: U.S. Census Bureau, *Children in Custody* Series. Washington, D.C. 1985.

against jails, the practice of jailing juveniles has ceased or has been severely curtailed. For example, Mark Soler, director of the Youth Law Center in San Francisco, and his associates have brought suits against fourteen jails in the past eight-and-a-half years. They have yet to lose a case, and all the decisions have resulted in either a ban on juvenile jailing or a limit on the offenses for which juveniles can be confined and an improvement in the conditions under which they are held. In 1982, Alan Bailey, director of the Juvenile Rights Project of the Oregon Legal Services Corporation in Portland, and his colleagues and staff from the National Center for Youth Law in St. Louis, brought suit against the Columbia County jail. The result was a federal court order banning the jailing of juveniles throughout the state.

A number of private, nonprofit, state-based advocacy groups have also had a significant impact on juvenile justice policies and practices in their respective states. The Massachusetts Advocacy Center has been a constructive critic of the youth corrections system in Massachusetts for years. It played an important role in helping to precipitate some of the reforms that have taken place in that state, and it continues to maintain a watchful eye over the system. Kentucky Youth Advocates (KYA) is another group that has made a difference. Its studies and reports of abuses in Kentucky's juvenile correctional facilities and adult jails have been influential in mobilizing support for change. KYA is considered to be a respected voice in the state and is unafraid to surface and speak out on controversial issues when necessary.

Florida is considered one of the most volatile states in the country with respect to juvenile justice policy. During the past two decades, there have been extreme shifts in Florida's approach to juvenile law violators, and recent policies rank among the most punitive in the country. Also, Florida's juvenile justice system has been characterized by abusive practices, some of which have been the subject of class action litigation and have been exposed in the media. Through all of this, the Florida Center for Children and Youth has been a consistent and forceful advocate for enlightened policies and practices. The Florida Center has earned the respect of key policy and decision makers in the state and has had a constructive impact in a difficult environment.

Discussion

The history of child advocacy in juvenile justice over the past twenty years has been a checkered one. Public interest attorneys attacked the conditions under which juveniles were being confined in institutions. Their efforts brought about important and desperately needed reforms.

Former senator Bayh orchestrated the movement that focused national public attention on the shortcomings of the juvenile justice system and mobilized the broad support needed among child advocacy organizations, public interest groups, professional associations, national youth-serving organizations, and the juvenile justice and child welfare communities to make juvenile justice reform a national priority.

Jerry Miller had the vision and, more important, the courage to dismantle an abusive and obsolete system and initiate a process that led to fundamental changes in Massachusetts' approach to handling juvenile offenders. This process led to an overhaul of the youth corrections system in that state, a system recognized nationally and internationally as one of the standard-bearers in the field.

A number of individuals and groups who are part of that history clearly did not measure up to the challenge, however. By and large, these were individuals and groups who had an enormous vested interest in maintaining the status quo, who became dependent upon and corrupted by the availability of federal juvenile justice funds, who were co-opted by the system, or who were influenced by some combination of these factors. Ironically, the federal juvenile justice funds that were supposed to help bring about reforms were used, in part, to strengthen and increase the capability of such groups as the National Council of Juvenile and Family Court Judges to influence youth policy at state and national levels. This organization, along with some of the others, has been indifferent, resisted, and attempted to undermine many of the needed changes in the juvenile justice system, some of which were embodied in the Juvenile Justice and Delinquency Prevention Act itself. They have also attracted funds that could have been more wisely invested elsewhere.

The reality is that the politics of juvenile justice at the national and state levels is no different from that in other areas (for example, health, education, transportation, economic development, and national security and defense). For example, special interest groups, particularly those who have been benefiting from the availability of federal juvenile justice funds since the OJJDP was created, tend to dominate what debate there is and have far too much influence over policy. Many of these groups are located in or close to Washington, D.C., with some having paid lobbyists to make sure that their interests are being looked after. Because of this, juvenile justice policy at the national, state, and local levels needs to be monitored, debated, and influenced by groups and organizations that are truly independent and are interested in seeing to it that juvenile crime prevention and control resources are being wisely invested. To a limited extent, this is being done by such groups as the League of Women Voters, the National Council of Jewish Women, and the Association of Junior Leagues, and by a few select state-level child advocacy groups. However, much more needs to be done in this area. In fact, all states could benefit from private, nonprofit, and privately financed organizations that would act as watchdogs over state and local juvenile justice policy. Such groups are needed to conduct special studies and issue reports and informed opinions on critical issues, to educate the public, and to attempt to influence juvenile justice policies, priorities, and the amount and allocation of resources.

Notes

1. National Council of Juvenile and Family Court Judges (undated).
2. Ibid.
3. Schoeller (1981).
4. Schoeller (1982).
5. Ibid.
6. Milligan (1982).
7. National Council of Juvenile and Family Court Judges (1981), p. 6.
8. Ibid., p. 5.
9. Kobrin and Klein (1980), p. 20.
10. Raley (1980), p. 4.
11. Ibid., pp. 4–5.
12. National Council of Juvenile and Family Court Judges (1985), p. 6.
13. Ibid., pp. 24–25.
14. *Resolution XXI* (1987).
15. *Child Protection Report* (1987), p. 2.
16. Marshall (1987), pp. 45–46.
17. Ibid., p. 46.
18. Steinhart, (1986).
19. Coates, Miller, and Ohlin (1978), p. 198.
20. *Hanna v. Toner* (1984).
21. *D. B. v. Tewksbury* (1982).

References

Child Protection Report XIII (16–17). 25 August 1987.

Coates, R.B.; Miller, A.D.; and Ohlin, L.E. 1978. *Diversity in a Youth Correctional System: Handling Delinquents in Massachusetts.* Cambridge, Mass.; Ballinger.

Kobrin, S., and Klein, M.W. 1980. *National Evaluation of the Deinstitutionalization of Status Offender Programs: Preliminary Executive Summary.* Washington, D.C.: unpublished document.

Marshall, T.O. 1987. "Building a Juvenile Justice System for Georgia's Future." In *Reinvesting Youth Corrections Resources: A Tale of Three States*, ed. L. Eddison. Minneapolis: University of Minnesota, Center for the Study of Youth Policy.

McHardy, L.W. 27 June 1986. Letter to the Editor, *The New Republic.*

Milligan, J.R. 28 October 1982. Memo to Wilkinson, Whitman, and Dobson.

National Council of Juvenile and Family Court Judges. 1981. *Bench Sense.* Reno: University of Nevada.

———. 1985. *Annual Report.* Reno, Nev.: Public Affairs Office of the National Council of Juvenile and Family Court Judges.

———. Undated. *To Help Protect* (pamphlet).

Raley, G. A. 9 May 1980. Memo to J. R. Milligan.

Resolution XXI, Jailing of Juveniles. August 1987. Adopted by Courts and Children's Committee, 39th Annual Meeting of the Conference of Chief Justices, Rapid City, South Dakota.

Schoeller, A. 20 February 1981. National Council of Juvenile and Family Court Judges, Inter-Council Memorandum.

————. 26 October 1982. National Council of Juvenile and Family Court Judges, Inter-Council Memorandum.

Steinhart, D. 9 September 1986. Memo to Interested Parties.

U.S. Census Bureau. 1979, 1984. *Children in Custody*, Washington, D.C.

Legal Cases

D.B. v. Tewksbury. 545 F. Supp. (D. Oregon 1982).
Hanna v. Toner. 1506 F. Supp. (D. Ohio 1984).

6

The Federal Role

WHEN President Jimmy Carter was defeated by Ronald Reagan in 1980, the word came down from the White House that President Carter didn't want a last-minute rush to complete or sneak through a lot of unfinished business before the new administration took office. Also, the Republicans were threatening to drag their feet on anything important, particularly issues that might have a long-range impact on public policy. I had never been in a politically appointed position before, and it was hard for me to come to grips with the fact that I was part of an administration that was being turned out by the voters. I was angry and depressed. I felt that I had done a respectable job as administrator, but more important, I felt that there were still more things I wanted to accomplish.

The reauthorization of the Juvenile Justice and Delinquency Prevention Act had yet to be completed. I knew that if the reauthorization wasn't completed and if President Carter didn't sign a new bill into law, there was a good chance that the federal juvenile justice program was finished.

I called a meeting of my closest and most trusted staff. We decided to put all of our time and energy into seeing that the act was reauthorized and signed by President Carter before President-elect Reagan took office. We developed a strategy aimed at mobilizing mainstream groups and organizations that traditionally supported the program and played such a key role in providing the support that was needed to create the program in the first place (for example, the PTA, the Association of Junior Leagues, the National Council of Jewish Women, Boys' Clubs of America, Girls' Clubs of America, the National League of Cities, the Campfire Girls, the United Way, the U.S. Conference of Mayors, the YMCA, the YWCA, the National Association of Counties).

The strategy worked. These groups put enormous pressure on Congress and, later, on the White House. The pressure was so intense that I got a call from Congressman Tip O'Neill's office to let me know that they were being flooded with letters, telegrams, and phone calls and to assure me that the Speaker would get the bill out of the House and on the president's desk.

A Sneak Preview of the Juvenile Justice Agenda for the Next Eight Years

The weeks following the 1980 national election continued to be difficult ones for me. I was concerned about what I was going to do after the Reagan administration took over as well as about whether we were going to be able to finish the reauthorization in time. There were rumors circulating in Washington, D.C., and throughout the country regarding who the next OJJDP "guru" (that is, my replacement) was going to be. I remember thinking, at the time, that many of the rumors were probably started by people who were interested in the job for themselves.

On December 8, 1980, the day President Carter signed the Juvenile Justice and Delinquency Prevention Act into law for another three years, I met with two members of the Reagan transition team who were assigned to the Department of Justice: Alfred S. Regnery and James H. Wentzel. Regnery was an aide to former senator Paul Laxalt, and Wentzel was an attorney in private practice in the district.

After we exchanged pleasantries, Regnery asked me what I thought about the "Ashbrook amendment," and about states that "disagreed with the Juvenile Justice and Delinquency Prevention Act's philosophy and were pro-family."

I told him that the act was not "antifamily" and that the valid court order, or Ashbrook amendment, was unnecessary. The administrative regulations put out by the OJJDP allowed status offenders to be detained in secure facilities for up to twenty-four hours, excluding weekends and holidays. This has proved to be adequate for handling those relatively few juveniles whose health and welfare was in danger and who refused to take advantage of voluntary social services. Also, for those juveniles who continue to be in danger, juvenile justice and child welfare officials could initiate action through existing state dependency and neglect statutes.

I explained that participation by the states in the federal juvenile justice program was voluntary and that, if anything, the act was designed to help keep children and families together or to reunite them if at all possible. I mentioned that it was important to remember that a substantial proportion of the youth who were incarcerated in adult jails, detention centers, and training schools in the early and mid-1970s were status offenders and, to a lesser extent, dependent, neglected, or abused children. These children were often mixed in with serious juvenile offenders or even with adult criminals. I discussed the horrors resulting from confining juveniles in adult jails and why it was important to end this practice.

Regnery then asked why I funded "advocacy groups that sued states." I told him that we funded legal groups to do a variety of things. They mainly provided consultation to states and counties in such areas as juvenile code revision, upgrading of juvenile justice standards, and prevention and correction of abusive and substandard professional practices. I emphasized that litigation was used only as a last resort, when all efforts to negotiate with and persuade officials to stop or correct such practices had failed. I explained that since states and counties are not likely to fund legal groups that might bring litigation against themselves, I felt that the office had a responsibility to ensure that when all reasonable efforts to eliminate abuses had failed, there would still be a way to protect children from being mistreated in institutions.

I could tell that Regnery did not agree with what I had to say. Wentzel didn't say much during the meeting; he looked bored and uninterested.

That night I wrote in my diary that I was visited by two members of the transition team. My impression was that "they didn't seem to care about kids." The next time I heard about Regnery was when he was appointed by Reagan to succeed me as head of the OJJDP. Little did I know that the meeting I had with him in December 1980 was a sneak preview of the national juvenile justice agenda for the next eight years. During his tenure as administrator, Regnery managed to repoliticize the office, mislead the American people, and practically destroy the credibility of the entire federal juvenile justice effort. He ended up resigning under fire.

I never knew what happened to James Wentzel. I recently read that he resigned as president of the Legal Services Corporation. The article indicated that Wentzel, who was appointed by President Reagan and was a former prosecutor in Colorado, "had been identified by a grocery store security official as a man apprehended for allegedly shoplifting $5.66 worth of food at a Northern Virginia supermarket."[1] The article indicated he resigned so that he could devote more time to resolving his "pending personal legal matters."[2]

The Politics of the Juvenile Justice and Delinquency Prevention Act of 1974

The federal government's role in juvenile delinquency dates back to the creation of the U.S. Children's Bureau in 1912.[3] However, all federal efforts in this area pale when compared to the Juvenile Justice and Delinquency Prevention Act of 1974. The act grew out of more than five years of inquiry into the juvenile justice system by the U.S. Senate Subcommittee to Investigate Juvenile Delinquency. The subcommittee, chaired by former U.S. senator Bayh of Indiana, conducted extensive hearings and heard from scores of witnesses, including juvenile court judges, youth corrections experts, academics, educators, child advocates, prosecutors, public defenders, parents, children, health care professionals, public interest groups, professional associations, and representatives from the media. They also visited juvenile correctional facilities and programs in a number of states.

The subcommittee found that large numbers of the juveniles confined in training schools, detention centers, and adult jails were status offenders, many of whom were "children who are victims of parental and societal neglect."[4] They found that "overcrowded, understaffed juvenile courts, probation services, and training schools, rarely have the time, energy, or resources to offer the individualized treatment which the juvenile justice system was designed to provide."[5] The subcommittee concluded: "The juvenile justice system is a failure, not only from the child's point of view but also from the point of view of our society."[6] Also, the subcommittee felt that the federal government could no longer ignore the fact that juveniles accounted for a substantial and disproportionate amount of serious crime and that federal leadership and resources were needed to help states and local units of government develop more effective juvenile crime prevention and control efforts.

Although there was general agreement about the need for the federal government to become more active in juvenile justice, there were two hurdles that needed to be overcome. There were major disagreements over which federal agency should house the new juvenile justice program. Also, President Ford was reluctant to start new federal programs, particularly with block grant funding to the states, because the administration and the Congress were facing a budget deficit.

The debate over the program's location was essentially between those who wanted it placed in the Law Enforcement Assistance Administration (LEAA) in the Department of Justice and those who favored some other agency in the federal bureaucracy. On February 8, 1973, Senators Birch Bayh of Indiana and Marlow W. Cook of Kentucky, both Democrats, introduced Senate Bill 821, which proposed creating a national office of juvenile justice and delinquency prevention in the executive office of the president.[7] This proposed office was modeled after the Special Action Office for Drug Abuse Prevention, created by President Nixon to respond to the crisis in drug abuse.[8]

Bayh was convinced that strong, centralized leadership over and coordination of all federal juvenile delinquency programs were needed.[9] He felt that housing the program in the Executive Office of the President would give it the necessary visibility and clout to bring this about.

The subcommittee held hearings on Senate Bill 821 during the winter and summer of 1973. The bill ran into stiff opposition from the administration as well as from key Republican members of the Senate. Administration officials from the LEAA and from the Department of Health, Education and Welfare (now the Department of Health and Human Services) testified against the bill.[10] Senator Roman Hruska of Nebraska, one of the Senate's most influential members and the "godfather" of the LEAA, felt that it was ill advised to consider creating a new categorical block grant program "at a time when general revenue sharing has just become operative." Hruska also expressed reservations about implementing a juvenile crime control program separate and apart from existing federal efforts.[11] Hruska was referring, of course, to the LEAA.

Faced with this opposition, Bayh amended the bill. The amended bill called for the establishment of a "Juvenile Justice and Delinquency Prevention Administration in the Department of Health, Education and Welfare."[12] Bayh preferred the Department of Health, Education and Welfare because he felt that that agency would emphasize delinquency prevention over juvenile court processing and reliance on incarceration. He felt that the LEAA was too concerned with such things as law enforcement equipment (for example, armored vehicles, riot control gear, police radios and helicopters) and prisons.

On May 8, 1974, the full Senate Judiciary Committee met to consider Senate Bill 821. Senator Hruska offered an amendment that, among other things, proposed creating an OJJDP that would be administered under the LEAA in the Department of Justice. The amendment passed by a vote of eight to five.[13]

On June 12, 1974, Representative Augustus Hawkins of California introduced HR 15276.[14] This was a companion bill to the one passed in the Senate, except that it placed the OJJDP in the Department of Health, Education and Welfare. Hawkins was adamant about keeping the program out of the Department of Justice. When he introduced the bill on the floor of the House, Hawkins stated:

> LEAA was considered and rejected by the [Subcommittee on Human Resources and the Committee on Education and Labor] . . . because of its narrow "cops and robbers" approach, its failure to adequately attend to the preventive aspects of juvenile delinquency, the spotty record of its state planning agencies in this area, its inability to coordinate juvenile delinquency programs effectively on either the federal, state, or local levels, and its view of the juvenile offender primarily in terms of crime and punishment.

Hawkins noted that of all the witnesses who testified at the hearing on juvenile justice, only one favored placing it in the LEAA.[15] When it became apparent that a juvenile justice bill was going to be enacted by Congress, officials from the White House and the Office of Management and Budget instructed bureaucrats from the Departments of Justice and Health, Education and Welfare to stay out of the dispute and let Congress decide where the program should be located. The Department of Justice officials felt that there was too much at stake, and they weren't about to let Congress make the decision all by itself. Almost from the very day they were ordered to stay out of the fight, staff from the administrator's and general counsel's offices of the LEAA worked behind the scenes. The LEAA administrator and general counsel assigned a member of their staff to be the liaison between the LEAA and Congress on this issue. The staff member, John Wilson, was new to the general counsel's staff, and no one knew who he was. His instructions were to do whatever he could to get the program located under the LEAA in the Department of Justice without it becoming known that he was representing the LEAA or the department in the process.

A House/Senate conference committee met in August 1974 to iron out their differences. Congressional staffers who were involved in the process recall that the Senate sent out its "big guns" and that it was a foregone conclusion that the Senate's version of the bill would prevail. Indeed, that proved to be the case. The Senate was represented by Senators Bayh of Indiana, John L. McClellan of Arkansas, Philip A. Hart of Michigan, Quentin N. Burdick of North Dakota, Roman Hruska of Nebraska, Hugh Scott of Pennsylvania, Marlow W. Cook of Kentucky, and Charles McC. Mathias, Jr., of Maryland. The House was represented by Carl D. Perkins of Kentucky, Augustus F. Hawkins of California, Shirley Chisholm of New York, and Albert H. Quie of Minnesota.

The bill that passed in the Senate included a section calling for the creation of a National Institute of Corrections (NIC) under the Federal Bureau of Prisons. Few people are aware of this; of those who are, many wonder why a program aimed at improving adult corrections was tacked on to the Juvenile Justice Act.

There are two scenarios for why this happened. Officials from the Federal Bureau of Prisons claim that the NIC would not have been created if it had been proposed in a separate bill. The administration and the Office of Management and Budget were against creating new programs and would have killed or vetoed it. Therefore, it was quietly added to the Juvenile Justice Act in the hope that no one in the White House or the Office of Management and Budget would notice it.

Another explanation is that the NIC proposal was tacked on in exchange for Republican senator Burdick's support. At the time, Senator Burdick was chair of the Subcommittee on Penitentiaries and Corrections, which had oversight responsibilities for the Bureau of Prisons. Burdick wanted the NIC, and he wanted it under the Bureau of Prisons.

The truth probably lies somewhere in between. The Juvenile Justice and Delinquency Prevention Act needed strong Republican support to have any chance of being signed into law by a Republican president who didn't want to start any new federal programs. As one insider put it, "Deals had to be cut." The National Institute of Corrections was a good concept, and it was one of those deals that could be consummated without having to "hold your nose" while it was being made.

The Juvenile Justice and Delinquency Prevention Act passed in the U.S. House by a vote of 329 to 20. It passed in the Senate with only one dissenting vote.[16] This meant that Congress had the votes to override a presidential veto in the event that President Ford chose to exercise it. Faced with this reality, Assistant Attorney General W. Vincent Rakestraw recommended in a letter to Roy L. Ash, director of the Office of Management and Budget, that the administration support the bill. Rakestraw pointed out that this was the first crime control legislation passed by Congress during the Ford administration. He emphasized that this was an opportunity for Ford to demonstrate his willingness to cooperate with Congress and, at the same time, join efforts in combating juvenile crime. He suggested that the Juvenile Justice and Delinquency Prevention Act was really not a "new federal program" but a restructuring and consolidation of and supplement to efforts already under way within the LEAA.[17] Rakestraw said that the bill had the backing of Republican senator Hruska, who had spoken to the bill on the floor of the Senate, emphasizing:

> [It] represents the culmination of years of hard work and the expertise and dedication of a great many individuals. The importance of this piece of legislation cannot be overstated. While we in government are attempting to achieve a balanced budget, certain crisis problems such as juvenile delinquency demand an immediate mobilization of Federal resources. The crisis of juvenile delinquency must be met.[18]

A reluctant President Ford signed the bill into law on September 7, 1974.[19]

Juvenile Justice: A National Priority

The Juvenile Justice and Delinquency Prevention Act was a victory for juvenile justice professionals, child advocates, and public interest groups. It meant that juvenile justice had finally become an important national priority and that the federal government would play a leadership role in helping to bring about change. Unfortunately, the fifteen-year history of the federal program shows how a broadly supported and landmark piece of legislation was translated into a program characterized by unfulfilled expectations, inept and revolving-door leadership, misplaced priorities, ill-conceived and foolish programs, scandals, and, more recently, a national embarrassment.

For eleven of the fifteen years that the program has been in existence, it has been under the control of hostile administrations. Presidents Ford and Reagan never requested any funds for the program from Congress. Ford didn't ask Congress for any money because of the budget deficit and he felt it necessary to increase expenditures for defense and energy conservation.[20] President Reagan has tried to "zero out" the program's budget every year since he's been in office. Like President Ford, Reagan has tried to kill the program because of the need to balance the budget, while he has ploughed more money into defense. The Reagan administration also asserts that the program is no longer needed because it has achieved its major objectives and because juvenile crime control is essentially a state and local problem.

The National Coalition of State Juvenile Justice Advisory Committees issued a report on the federal juvenile justice program in April 1986. Although the track record of many of these committees is spotty in terms of championing the cause of juvenile justice reform, the report, in my opinion, contains an accurate and candid assessment of the OJJDP's leadership and its program's performance. The coalition noted:

> Since September 1974, OJJDP has had eight administrators—four presidential appointees, and four acting administrators. In the 11 years since the Act became law, acting administrators have been responsible for the operation of the office for almost half the time. A lack of continuity and ambiguity of purpose has made it virtually impossible for any single set of policies or strategies to survive."[21]

The program has had one additional administrator since this report was issued. The problems the coalition identified are ones that have characterized Republican and Democratic administrations alike. For example, the coalition pointed out:

> [T]wo of the most controversial administrators of the office [John Rector and Alfred S. Regnery] . . . [had] much in common, even though one was a Democrat and one was a Republican. Both owe their appointments to having been staff aides on Capitol Hill, and both came to the office without work experience in juvenile justice. Both viewed the office as a vehicle for implementing their own ideologies. Both funded numerous projects that had the appearance of being outside the spirit, if not the letter of the law; hence the "lawless" reference was coined to describe the office.[22]

For example, Regnery approved a grant for $734,371 to study how children were depicted in cartoons in *Hustler*, *Penthouse*, and *Playboy* magazines. The purpose of the grant was to try to determine whether the cartoons had an impact on abnormal sexual behavior in children and on child pornography.[23] Regnery also gave $186,710 to James McClellan—a conservative activist who is on the faculty at Reverend Jerry Falwell's Liberty College in Virginia—to write high school curriculum materials on the Constitution from a "conservative's" point of view. McClellan, a former aid to Republican senators Jesse Helms of North Carolina and Orrin Hatch of Utah, is known for his criticisms of the courts for using the "First Amendment to prohibit school prayer and other religious activities. He was an expert witness for Alabama authorities in a case in which the Supreme Court struck down a 'moment of silence' in the state's schools."[24]

Other problems have also hampered the program. Congressional oversight has been inconsistent and weak, which has helped create the conditions that allowed administrators of the office to operate without an effective system of checks and balances. Some of the problems that have hindered the program are ones to which only an insider could be privy. I will never forget the meeting I had with attorney general designate Benjamin Civiletti before I was nominated by President Carter to serve as administrator. At the meeting, Civiletti indicated that my predecessor, John Rector, had lost the confidence and trust of top officials in the Department of Justice. I subsequently learned that this loss of credibility had adversely affected Rector's ability to manage the program. I felt bad about this, because John Rector, when he served as the deputy chief and eventually chief counsel to the Senate Subcommittee on Juvenile Delinquency, had played a crucial role in the development of the Juvenile Justice and Delinquency Prevention Act of 1974. As Senator Bayh recalls, "John knew when to be tough and when it was necessary to compromise in order to get something done."[25]

Another serious problem that plagued the program from its inception was that the major actors always seemed to get locked into implementing a narrow agenda. This, too, was a problem that characterized both Democratic and Republican administrations.

The "Liberal" Agenda

The Juvenile Justice and Delinquency Prevention Act of 1974 had a definite reform thrust. However, in their zeal to get the legislation enacted, the supporters of the act—as well as some of the members of Congress who made it a reality—paid insufficient attention to the problem of serious juvenile crime. This was also true of those, including myself, who were responsible for implementing the program between 1974 and 1980. There were always references to the fact that juveniles accounted for a substantially disproportionate amount of serious crime. Upon reflection, however, it seems that this was mainly used as a convenient justification for the need for the program, rather than as an impetus for doing something about serious and violent juvenile crime.

For example, the Juvenile Justice and Delinquency Prevention Act mainly called upon the federal government to provide

> the necessary resources, leadership and coordination (1) to develop and implement effective methods of preventing and reducing delinquency; (2) to develop and conduct effective programs to prevent delinquency, to divert juveniles from the traditional juvenile justice system, and to provide critically needed alternatives to institutionalization; and (3) to improve the quality of juvenile justice in the United States.[26]

The principal objectives of the act are to promote the deinstitutionalization of status offenders and dependent, neglected, and abused
children; to encourage the elimination of the practice of jailing
juveniles; and to encourage the development of "community-based
alternatives to juvenile detention and correctional facilities."[27] Although the authors of the legislation acknowledged that "some
youthful offenders must be removed from their communities for
society's sake as well as their own," this population was not a priority
prior to 1980.[28]

The most telling indicator of the lack of attention paid to this issue
is the fact that less than 10 percent of the nearly $120 million in
discretionary funds given out by the OJJDP between 1975 and 1980
was targeted for violent and chronic juvenile offenders.[29] Serious
juvenile crime became a priority only after Congress started putting
some heat on the OJJDP for ignoring the issue.[30]

The lack of priority and attention given to the serious juvenile
crime problem was a major political blunder. It indicated that at a
time when public concern about juvenile crime was at a fever pitch
and state policymakers and juvenile justice professionals were getting
tough with juvenile law violators, the federal government was not
only insensitive to the issue but was essentially emphasizing an
entirely different agenda. This hurt the credibility of the program
and laid the groundwork for some of the changes that were to come
in the years ahead.

The New Agenda

The federal juvenile justice agenda shifted dramatically when the
Reagan administration came to power. The new agenda attacked the
mandates in the Juvenile Justice and Delinquency Prevention Act
that were viewed as "antifamily" and called for cracking down on
juvenile law violators. In their zeal to implement this new agenda,
Reagan administration officials turned their backs on the need for
reform, put out inaccurate and misleading information, and either
ignored or tried to influence research findings that didn't support
their policies or point of view.

The clearest and most comprehensive expression of the new
agenda appears in the report *Serious Juvenile Crime: A Redirected
Federal Effort.* This report, which was submitted to the president and

the Congress, was prepared by the now defunct presidentially appointed National Advisory Committee for Juvenile Justice and Delinquency Prevention. The committee felt that "the time has come for a major departure from existing philosophy and activity of the federal government in the juvenile justice field."[31] Committee members acknowledged the importance of such objectives as removing status offenders from secure facilities and encouraging the separation of juveniles from adult offenders in correctional institutions. However, they emphasized that these are largely state and local concerns, and they questioned whether they were appropriate activities for the federal government to be engaged in. The committee recommended that the "federal effort in the area of juvenile delinquency should focus primarily on the serious, violent, or chronic offender."[32] The committee also recommended that the federal government play a role in such areas as research, designing and evaluating demonstration projects of national significance, disseminating information, and providing technical assistance and training.[33]

The Assault on Status Offenders

After being confirmed as administrator of the OJJDP in 1982, Alfred S. Regnery launched a systematic and aggressive campaign to undercut the act's mandates regarding status offenders. This was the part of the legislation he and some others in and outside the administration considered "antifamily." In 1984, the OJJDP released a report entitled *Runaway Children and the Juvenile Justice and Delinquency Prevention Act: What Is the Impact?* The publication contains a series of horror stories about children, mainly girls, who ran away from home and got involved with drugs and prostitution. Regnery wrote the introduction to the piece, which he asserted that "Congress effectively tied the hands of juvenile authorities, leaving runaways, quite literally, out in the cold."[34] The result was that "deinstitutionalization has emancipated children, essentially allowing them to live wherever and however they choose." He also asserted that "deinstitutionalization has too often meant, not transferring youth from reform schools to caring environments but releasing them to the exploitation of the streets."[35]

Regnery also felt that the federal policies regarding status offenders were misguided because "not only does running away lead to illegal behavior—illegal behavior which may be necessary for survival—but it often leads to more serious offenses."[36] In 1986, he remarked that runaways end up being " 'throwaways' . . . [and] often become involved in prostitution, pornography, drug dealing, numbers running, and whatever other activities from which they can squeeze out an existence."[37] To bolster his argument, Regnery claimed that "1.2 million children under sixteen are engaged in prostitution" in the United States.[38] He felt that status offenders were victims or were in danger of becoming victimized and that dealing with them "has been hampered by laws that curtail the authority of both law enforcement agencies to arrest runaway youth and the juvenile court to detain them."[39]

Obviously, federal policies should not be viewed as permanent. They should be periodically reexamined and, when called for, modified. However, as my initial contact with Regnery when he was a member of the Reagan transition team revealed, Regnery's mind was made up even before he took over the reigns of the office. He believed that prohibiting the incarceration of runaways, habitual truants, and youth in conflict with their parents was "antifamily." He ignored the available research on the topic, and even worse, he distorted the facts to fit his personal point of view.

For example, Solomon Kobrin and Malcolm W. Klein conducted a national evaluation of deinstitutionalization of status offender programs. They conclude that given "the current 'state of the art' neither juvenile justice processing nor deinstitutionalization in status offense cases offers delinquency control advantages over the other, although the latter may afford some cost reduction."[40] In another important study, Joseph G. Weis and his associates found that juveniles "who begin their offender careers engaging in status offenses only [or in petty illegal behavior]" are not likely to graduate into more serious crime.[41]

Regnery's source for the number of teenage prostitutes is a 1982 General Accounting Office study entitled *Sexual Exploitation: A Problem of Unknown Magnitude*. The report indicates that the estimates of the number of teenage prostitutes in the United States are "based on 'gut hunches.' "[42] Regnery chose to use the highest and most crudely developed of the estimates in the entire report.

The Missing and Exploited Children Connection

Each year, a small number of children in the United States are murdered. Some children are kidnapped by strangers; they are often physically and sexually abused, and sometimes the are killed by their abductors. A much larger but unknown number of children are abducted each year by one of their parents. These are usually situations in which the parents are in the midst of getting a divorce or are divorced and are in a war with each other over the custody of their children. No words can adequately describe the anguish and pain these children and their parents experience. To their credit, officials in the OJJDP and in the Department of Justice in the Reagan administration became sensitized to these issues and brought them to the attention of the American people.

Unfortunately, Reagan administration officials also exploited this issue, in part, to further their efforts to gut the federal juvenile justice program. They claimed that the prohibitions against locking up status offenders undermined the ability of parents to control their children effectively. They maintained that the estimated more than one million children who run away from home every year are particularly high-risk candidates for being kidnapped or murdered by strangers or sexually exploited. Once again, there was a barrage of exaggerated statistics and unsupported claims. This time the result was more serious, because "this misplaced activism transformed a problem of very limited scope into a pseudo-crisis."[43]

This "misplaced activism" had a particularly significant impact on children. A recent national youth attitude survey conducted by the Roper Organization revealed that the issue of greatest concern to children between the ages of 8 and 17 is being kidnapped by a stranger. Concern about being abducted by a stranger loomed larger than concerns about the possibility of nuclear war, the spread of AIDS, drug abuse by professional athletes, childhood accidents and diseases, divorce among parents, and so on.[44]

The OJJDP pumped millions of dollars into creating an organization called the National Center for Missing and Exploited Children, an organization whose staff and consultants put out inflated, misleading, and unsubstantiated figures on the number of children who are abducted by strangers or who end up truly missing each year. Pictures of missing children surfaced on milk cartons and envelopes, in taxi cabs and bowling alleys, on television, and even in Congress. Parents were encouraged to bring their children to shopping malls to have them fingerprinted. Advertisements appeared on television encouraging parents to call a number and, for a small fee, hear information on how to protect their children.

As concerns for missing and exploited children were sweeping the country, the media began to look into the numbers. When they checked with local law enforcement agencies, the FBI, and small nonprofit organizations that help find missing children, they discovered huge discrepancies between the figures they dug up and those coming out of the federal government and its creature, the National Center for Missing and Exploited Children. The *Denver Post*, after an exhaustive investigation, ran a series of articles in May 1985 entitled "Exaggerated Statistics Stir National Paranoia." The articles, for which the *Denver Post* won a Pulitzer Prize, alerted others to the facts. The *Denver Post* reporters found out, among other things, that the overwhelming majority of children who are kidnapped each year are abducted by one of their own parents. Similar accounts have also appeared in other media investigations from coast to coast.

In December 1984, Regnery wrote that status offenders were among the "estimated 2,000 unidentified children's bodies buried annually by police."[45] During the same year, the College of American Pathologists surveyed its membership to determine the number of unidentified children who had died from all causes. Based on the survey results, they estimated that the maximum number of unidentified dead children nationwide was less than 200.[46] Moreover, the FBI reported that in 1983, 897 children 15 years of age or younger were murdered in the United States. Most of these children were killed at the hands of their own parents, other family members, or acquaintances—not by strangers.

In addition, and despite the absence of any credible evidence supporting their position, Attorney General Edwin Meese's Task Force on Missing and Exploited Children observed that "by mandating non-detention and non-secure holding intervention by police and juvenile courts, the Act fostered and encouraged the very result it sought to avoid—the tragedy of more and more children who are out of parental control."[47] Accordingly, the task force recommended that "Congress should amend the Juvenile Justice and Delinquency Prevention Act to ensure that each state juvenile justice system has the legal authority, where necessary and appropriate, to take in custody and safely control runaway and homeless children."[48]

Alfred Regnery left the Reagan administration in 1987, resigning from his position as administrator of the OJJDP in the midst of looming scandals and embarrassing media accounts regarding his tenure of office and his personal life.[49] Some people who were close to the situation at the time say that Regnery was forced to resign because he had become an embarrassment and a liability to the White House. Regnery was replaced by Verne Spiers. Although Spiers has been maintaining a low profile, there is evidence that he is every bit as political and ideological as Regnery. There are already rumors and some evidence that he is keeping information that is not in tune with administration philosophy from being disseminated (for example, the NCCD study of the youth corrections reforms in Utah) and that his is keeping enlightened and respected juvenile justice officials whose views may conflict with the administration's philosophy from participating in OJJDP-sponsored activities (for example, meetings, research and programmatic advisory committees, review panels).

The Administration Wants the Facts Out

On September 9, 1986, an announcement appeared in the *Federal Register* that the OJJDP was making $1 million available to be awarded on a "competitive" basis for "research on the effects of deinstitutionalization of status offenders." The announcement read:

> Given the tremendous amount of energy and resources that have been committed to DSO (Deinstitutionalization of Status Offenders), OJJDP feels it is necessary to systematically examine the positive and negative impact that deinstitutionalization of status offenders has had on youth, both in terms of risk of exploitation and subsequent delinquency and on youth-serving public institutions and private agencies.[50]

Incredibly, the feds would now have us believe that after Regnery spent several years trying to reverse federal policies on status offenders, and after Attorney General Meese's Task Force on Missing and Exploited Children declared that these policies were counterproductive, they are interested in an honest assessment of the impact federal mandates have had in this area.

The OJJDP also awarded a two-year $850,000 grant to study how many cases of missing children are actually reported to the police and how these cases are handled. Again, after Reagan administration officials exploited this issue to try to undermine congressional policies with which they disagree, triggering a national hysteria in the process, they want people to believe that they are now genuinely interested in determining the precise nature and scope of this problem.

The potential credibility of these efforts is stretched further because of the OJJDP's recent history of either ignoring or trying to influence research findings. For example, the Consortium of Social Science Associations reported:

> [Regnery] consistently misrepresented the data on juvenile crime trends. Even though data from the F.B.I.'s Uniform Crime Reports indicate crime rates for juveniles declined from 1976–1981, Regnery continued to talk about a juvenile crime wave in order to justify his position on incarcerating kids. The studies demonstrating the decline in crime "never saw the light of day."[51]

The consortium also reported:

> Although most researchers [they interviewed] noted that they had never been "explicitly pressured" into altering conclusions, a number suggested that the pressure was implicit. One called it a "self-censorship"—implied threats with unstated reprisals if the results were not congruent with the ideological goals of the office, i.e., taking a hard line towards juvenile criminals. One researcher did say his work had been edited without his knowledge because his attitude was "too liberal."[52]

Discussion

The Juvenile Justice and Delinquency Prevention Act of 1974 is the most important piece of federal juvenile justice legislation ever enacted. Despite the troubled history of the federal juvenile justice program, federal leadership is still needed to encourage necessary improvements in the quality of justice for children; to assist in advancing knowledge for preventing or controlling serious juvenile crime; to provide technical assistance and consultation to state and local policymakers, professionals, and public interest groups; and to inform and educate the public.

However, if the act is to remain viable and meet the challenges in the decades ahead, a number of changes need to be made in the legislation and in the way the program is administered. For example:

1. Congress should mandate that states receiving federal juvenile justice funds adhere to appropriate constitutional and generally accepted professional standards for the care and treatment of children under the custody and control of state and local juvenile justice systems. This would help ensure that children are adequately housed in public and private juvenile detention and correctional facilities; that they are safe and free from harm by staff and other youth; that they receive adequate health, education, and other appropriate services; and that their constitutional rights are not being violated.

2. The block grant program has proved to be a useful tool for bringing about needed reforms. There wouldn't have been any progress to speak of with respect to removing children from adult jails and police lockups if Congress hadn't made it a requirement for receiving federal juvenile justice funds. Although removing children from jails and lockups should remain a top priority, the block grant program should continue to be used as an incentive to encourage states to make other advances as well. In particular, Congress should amend the act, requiring states to upgrade and improve the quality of justice for children.

3. Congress should require that at least 80 percent of the discretionary funds be given out on a competitive basis. The authority in the act that gives the administrator of the OJJDP complete control over the disbursement of discretionary funds is too broad and, as has been demonstrated, can easily lead to abuses. Also, the discretionary funds should generally be used for research, for technical assistance and training, and for research-based demonstration programs that are likely to have significant national implications.

4. There must be more effective oversight over the federal juvenile justice program on the part of both the Senate and the House. Also, the Senate must take its advice and consent role far

more seriously in the future than it has in the past when the president nominates someone to serve as administrator of the OJJDP.

5. Although the OJJDP has absorbed large cuts in its budget, along with other federal domestic programs, the Congress and whatever administration is in power needs to face the fact that additional resources are required if desperately needed reforms are to be realized.

6. One of the most potentially significant and most neglected components of the Juvenile Justice and Delinquency Prevention Act is the section of the law creating a Coordinating Council on Juvenile Justice and Delinquency Prevention. The act requires that virtually all federal agencies involved with children and youth be members of the Coordinating Council and that they be represented by agency heads (for example, secretary of health and human services, secretary of education, commissioner of Bureau of Indian Affairs, director of the ACTION Agency). Further, the act specifies that the attorney general of the United States serve as the chair of the Coordinating Council and that the administrator of the OJJDP serve as vice-chair.[53]

The Coordinating Council is supposed to be the vehicle at the national level for reviewing and coordinating all federal juvenile delinquency policies, resources, and programs. It is supposed to serve as a forum for examining critical issues regarding juvenile delinquency prevention, control, and treatment; for developing priorities for action; and for promoting interagency planning and collaboration. It is also supposed to be a mechanism for identifying federal policies and practices that may conflict with the Juvenile Justice Act and for resolving these differences. Moreover, the Coordinating Council is supposed to advise both the president and the Congress on the role of the federal government on matters relating to juvenile delinquency and on how existing federal efforts can be improved.[54]

Clearly, a group composed of the heads of all the federal agencies that in some way affect the lives of children has enormous potential for wielding power and influence. It can cut through bureaucratic red tape and can have the capacity to tackle problems confronting youth comprehensively and effectively.

The problem with the Coordinating Council is that it has never been taken seriously. Republican and Democratic administrations alike have largely ignored the council, except when they wanted to make a big splash by announcing some new federal initiative involving more than one agency or when there was some political advantage to having a meeting.

The next president should take advantage of this "sleeping giant." The Coordinating Council represents a significant opportunity for bringing the resources of the federal bureaucracy together to focus on the problem of juvenile crime prevention and control. However, if this "sleeping giant" is to be properly activated and have a real impact, the next president must make sure that his or her attorney general knows about the Coordinating Council's existence and is instructed to implement the council's broad mandate to the fullest extent.

Notes

1. *Washington Post* (1986).
2. Ibid.
3. Law Enforcement Assistance Administration (1974), p. 1.
4. U.W. Congress, Senate, Committee on the Judiciary (1973), p. 45.
5. Ibid., p. 44.
6. Ibid.
7. Ibid., p. 326.
8. Ibid., p. 359.
9. Ibid., p. 358.
10. Ibid., pp. 669, 745.
11. Ibid., p. 634.
12. LEAA (1974), p. 2.
13. Ibid., p. 218.
14. Ibid., p. 4.
15. Ibid., pp. 92–93.
16. U.S. Congress, Senate, Committee on the Judiciary (1975), p. 7.
17. Rakestraw (1974).
18. Ibid.
19. LEAA (1974), p. 440.
20. U.S. Congress, Senate, Committee on the Judiciary (1975), Testimony of R.W. Velde, administrator of the LEAA, pp. 38–39.
21. National Coalition of State Juvenile Justice Advisory Committees (1986), pp. 2–3.
22. Ibid., pp. 12–13.
23. *Washington Times* (1986).
24. *Washington Post* (1986).

25. Schwartz (1987).
26. U.S. Congress, Senate, Committee on the Judiciary (1975), p. xii.
27. Ibid., p. xxi.
28. U.S. Congress, Senate, Committee on the Judiciary (1978), p. 49.
29. National Advisory Committee for Juvenile Justice and Delinquency Prevention (1984), p. 18.
30. U.S. Congress, Senate, Committee on the Judiciary (1978), p. 60.
31. National Advisory Committee for Juvenile Justice and Delinquency Prevention (1984), p. iii.
32. Ibid., p. 9.
33. Ibid., p. 11.
34. Office of Juvenile Justice and Delinquency Prevention (1984), p. 2.
35. Ibid., p. 9.
36. Regnery (1985), p. 3.
37. Regnery (1986), p. 14.
38. OJJDP (1984), p. 2.
39. Regnery (1986), pp. 14–15.
40. Kobrin and Klein (1982), p. 35.
41. Weis et al. (1980), p. 96.
42. U.S. General Accounting Office (1982), p. iv.
43. *Wall Street Journal* (1986).
44. American Chicle Youth Poll (1987), p. 19.
45. OJJDP (1984), p. 2.
46. College of American Pathologists,undated, p. 4.
47. U.S. Attorney General's Advisory Board on Missing Children (1986), 15.
48. Ibid., p. 19.
49. *New Republic* (1986); *Reason* (1986).
50. *Federal Register* (1986), p. 32184.
51. Consortium of Social Science Associations (1986), p. 4.
52. Ibid., p. 5.
53. U.S. Congress, House, Subcommittee on Human Resources (1980), p. 373.
54. Ibid.

References

American Chicle Youth Poll. March 1987. "A Landmark Study on the Attitudes of American Youth." Morris Plains, N.J.: Warner-Lambert Company.

College of American Pathologists. Undated. *Summary, College of American Pathologists Missing Children Project Survey*. n.pl. College of American Pathologists.

Consortium of Social Science Associations (COSSA). 1986. "Research Abuses Alleged at OJJDP." *COSSA Washington Update* 5 (12): 4–5.

Federal Register 51 (174). 1986.

Kobrin, S., and Klein, M.W. 1982. *National Evaluation of the Deinstitutionalization of Status Offender Programs: Executive Summary*. Washington, D.C.: U.S. Government Printing Office.

Law Enforcement Assistance Administration (LEAA), U.S. Department of Justice. 1974. *Indexed Legislative History of the Juvenile Justice and Delinquency Prevention Act of 1974*. Washington, D.C.: U.S. Government Printing Office.

National Advisory Committee for Juvenile Justice and Delinquency Prevention. 1984. *Serious Juvenile Crime: A Redirected Federal Effort*. Washington, D.C.: U.S. Department of Justice.

National Coalition of State Juvenile Justice Advisory Groups. 1986. *The First Report to the President, the Congress and the Administrator of the Office of Juvenile Justice and Delinquency Prevention*. Washington, D.C.

New Republic. 23 June 1986. "Al Regnery's Secret Life," pp. 16–19.

Office of Juvenile Justice and Delinquency Prevention (OJJDP), U.S. Department of Justice. 1984. *Runaway Children and the Juvenile Justice and Delinquency Prevention Act: What Is the Impact?* Juvenile Justice Bulletin. Washington, D.C.: U.S. Department of Justice.

Rakestraw, V. 23 August 1974. Letter to Roy L. Ash.

Reason. April 1986. "Reagan's Smutstompers," pp. 26–33.

Regnery, A.S. 1985. "The Deinstitutionalization of Status Offenders: It's Time to Analyze the JJDP Act Mandate." *Juvenile Justice Digest* 13(6): 1–5.

Regnery, A.S. 16 January 1986. "National Trends in the Juvenile Justice System." Speech given at the Minnesotans for Improved Juvenile Justice Conference, Minneapolis.

Schwartz I.M. 18 February 1987. Interview with Birch Bayh.

U.S. Attorney General's Advisory Board on Missing Children. 1986. *America's Missing and Exploited Children: Their Safety and Their Future*. Washington, D.C.: U.S. Department of Justice.

U.S. Congress, House, Committee on Education and Labor, Subcommittee on Human Resources. 19 March 1980. *Juvenile Justice Amendments of 1980*. 96th Cong., 2d sess.

U.S. Congress, Senate, Committee on the Judiciary, Subcommittee to Investigate Juvenile Delinquency. 1973. *The Juvenile Justice and Delinquency Prevention Act— S.3148 and S.821*. 92d Cong., 2d sess.; 93d Cong., 1st sess.

———. 1975. *Ford Administration Stifles Juvenile Justice Program*. 94th Cong., 1st sess.

———. 1978. *Serious Youth Crime*. 95th Cong., 2d sess.

U.S. General Accounting Office. 1982. *Sexual Exploitation of Children: A Problem of Unknown Magnitude*. Report to the Chairman, Subcommittee on Select Education and House Committee on Education and Labor. Washington, D.C.: General Accounting Office.

Wall Street Journal. 7 May 1986. "Where Are the Children?"

Washington Post. 16 December 1986. "Wentzel Resigns as Legal Services Corp. President."

Washington Times. 27 March 1986. "Official says $734,371 to Peer at Porn was wasteful."

Weis, J.G.; Sakumoto, K.; Sederstrom, J.; and Zeiss, C. 1980. *Jurisdiction and the Elusive Status Offender: A Comparison of Involvement in Delinquent Behavior and Status Offenses*. Washington, D.C.: U.S. Government Printing Office.

7

Being Abused at Better Prices

THE removal of status offenders from institutions in the juvenile justice system was one of the major objectives of the Juvenile Justice and Delinquency Prevention Act of 1974. Now it appears that many of these youth are being committed to a different kind of institution: inpatient psychiatric and chemical dependency units in private for-profit and nonprofit hospitals. Running away from home, habitual truancy, and being in conflict with one's parents are now being classified as emotional and psychiatric disorders—a process Patricia Guttridge calls the "medicalization of defiance."

The Case of Sandra

Sandra awoke from a deep sleep, confused and not knowing where she was. The walls were bare and unfamiliar. She looked around and was startled to see men wearing smocks, standing outside the door to her room and looking in.

She suddenly remembered where she was. She was in a hospital psychiatric unit. Sandra was frightened at the thought, because she remembered being locked in her room at bedtime by one of the staff. Now the door was wide open.

The day before, Sandra had gotten into a heated argument with her parents. She had wanted to go out with her girlfriends, but her parents had refused to let her. The argument ended when Sandra screamed, "I'm going to kill myself," and ran out of the house.

Sandra ran to the neighborhood convenience store. She tried to call her parents to apologize and to let them know that she was okay. She had never intended to kill herself—she had threatened to do so only because she "wasn't winning" the fight with her parents.

Sandra dialed the number several times, but the line was busy. She finally gave up and started to walk home. On her way home, Sandra was stopped by two police officers in a patrol car. They asked her to identify herself, and then one of the officers radioed for an ambulance, which took her to a nearby hospital.

Sandra was locked up in the psychiatric unit for seventy-two hours. She was not allowed to see or talk to her parents, even though they tried to see her on several occasions. While on the unit, Sandra rarely left her room. She was afraid to walk around, because there were adult male patients walking around. Also, she felt embarrassed because she was given only a "skimpy" hospital gown to wear.

Sandra is 15 years old. She's a good student, has never been in trouble with the law, and has no prior history of serious emotional or psychiatric disorders. Sandra has never run away from home and has not experimented with or used illegal drugs.

Sandra was a victim of the "hidden" system of juvenile control, but she was luckier than most. The overwhelming majority of children who get caught up in this system are incarcerated for weeks, months, and sometimes years before they are released.

We Can Fix Your Kids

Being a parent today is no picnic. Drugs and alcohol are readily available. Teenage pregnancy has reached epidemic proportions. More than one million children run away from home each year. The rate of teenage suicide is at an alarming level.

Traditionally, these problems have been addressed by elected public officials, child welfare professionals, school officials, health care professionals, the juvenile courts, child advocacy groups, youth-serving agencies, and public interest groups. They are now attracting the attention of the health care industry, particularly the large commercial health care conglomerates and administrators of private general hospitals that are confronted with empty beds and declining revenues. The result is that these organizations are getting into the inpatient psychiatric and chemical dependency (alcohol and drug abuse) treatment business as fast as they can. Mark Schlesinger, research coordinator for the Center for Health Care Policy Studies at Harvard, recently reported that approximately 1,000 short-term general hospitals are on the brink of getting into the inpatient psychiatric business.[1] The pressures to fill empty beds, coupled with the availability of third-party health care insurance programs with fiscal incentives that favor inpatient rather than outpatient care, are contributing to the proliferation of services that are largely inappropriate and costly.

The health care industry is proving to be particularly skilled in converting the concerns and fears of parents into huge profits. Unfortunately, the movement of the health care industry into providing psychiatric and chemical dependency services for youth is not always accompanied by business and professional practices that meet the highest standards. The intense competition between health care providers to capture a certain share of the "market" is contributing to Madison Avenue advertising techniques that are sometimes misleading and designed to both scare and take advantage of parents. Television, newspaper, and magazine ads now claim that hospitals can cure anything from failing grades and running away from home to drug addiction and alcoholism.

The ads often convey the message that parents aren't at fault or even a significant factor in their child's behavior—a message many parents want to hear. They suggest that such things as running away from home and delinquency are signs of depression or some other emotional disturbance. They imply that if parents don't act immediately to correct these problems, the problems will probably worsen, and their child may end up scarred for life or behind bars or may even commit suicide.

For example, a newspaper ad for the Fair Oaks Hospital in Del Rey Beach, Florida—a hospital owned by Psychiatric Institutes of America, a subsidiary of National Medical Enterprises, Inc.— pictures a teenage girl hitchhiking. The ad's bold print reads, "If you think living with your difficult child is tough, try living without her." The rest of the ad reads:

> Last year a million teenagers ran away from home. Running away is often a symptom of depression—a disease that can be treated.
> If you think your teenager is suffering from depression—don't

blame yourself or hope the problem will disappear. Call Fair Oaks Hospital. Before your child's problem gets beyond your reach.[2]

In January 1987, a newspaper ad for the Adolescent Health Program of the Golden Valley Health Center—a Minneapolis suburban facility that is part of the Comprehensive Care Corporation chain—appeared, picturing a boy sitting on a suitcase alongside a highway. The ad implied that most of the children who run away from home may never return. The ad suggested that running away may be caused by stress, particularly by peers and parents, and could lead to depression, delinquency, and even suicide. The ad encouraged parents to contact the hospital before it was too late.[3]

The implication is that most youths who run away from home never return is simply inaccurate. The best available evidence indicates that more than 95 percent of the juveniles who run away from home return within a few days. Also, the ad encourages parents to bring their children in if they are under "stress"—hardly a well-defined, serious psychiatric disorder that requires hospitalization.

After seeing the Golden Valley Health Center ad, I wrote a letter to them requesting documentation for their claim that most of the children who run away from home keep on running. I mentioned that it was my understanding that the overwhelming majority of children who run away from home return within a matter of few days. I received a reply from the Golden Valley Health Center's director, indicating that it was not their intention to mislead people and that they would change the ad.[4] The ad reappeared and, to their credit, they took out the misleading references to runaway children. However, the ad still encourages parents to hospitalize their children for "stress."

Paid advertising isn't the only method used by hospitals to recruit business. They also send out public relations and marketing staff to make direct appeals for referrals to school social workers and guidance counselors, teachers, and staff of youth-serving organizations. A staff member from a Boys' Club in Minneapolis told me he was routinely solicited for business by staff from a number of hospitals. He said that the hospital representatives would explain their programs to him and emphasize that they were designed to help young people get their lives back in order. They asked him to refer to them youth exhibiting behavior problems in the Boys' Clubs or youth he knew were having problems at home. Invariably, the hospital representatives indicated that they would appreciate knowing whether the mother or father of a potential patient was working and whether she or he had the kind of job that would provide insurance coverage. He said that they didn't seem particularly interested in getting referrals of children from poor families or of those whose families were on some form of public assistance. He also said that they didn't seem particularly interested in getting minority youth as clients.

It's clear to me that hospitals aren't rushing to get into this business out of the goodness of their hearts or because there's a well-documented need for significantly greater inpatient psychiatric and chemical dependency services for youth. They are getting into it because there's money to be made. For example, the *Wall Street Journal* reported that Community Psychiatric Centers had a 25 percent increase in profits for the quarter ending May 31, 1985. The article indicated that the growth in profits was largely due to "an increase in the use of its psychiatric services, which account for 75% of its business."[5] In 1986, Charter Medical Corporation generated gross revenues of $803.2 million. Charter's net income for that year was a tidy $43.7 million. Most of the company's revenues (52 percent) came from the operation of psychiatric hospitals.[6]

A Rand Corporation study found that "the treatment of drug abuse is a significant industry in the United States. In 1982, there were more than 3,000 treatment facilities, accounting for over $500 million in expenditures."[7] A recent article in the *New York Times* indicated that "companies are spending 7 to 15 percent of health-care dollars on psychiatric care, with drug and alcohol cases absorbing more than a third of this. These costs are rising steeply, even as health-care cost containment in general takes hold."[8]

Dr. Rodney L. Lowman is a well-known health care consultant. It was reported that he recently helped "a large, self-insured corporation get a handle on its health-care costs." Lowman discovered "that the company had spent $1.5 million in one year on 23 mental health-related cases—an average of more than $65,000 per case." In examining these cases, Lowman found that only one of the cases involved an employee of the company, one case involved the spouse of a company employee, and "21 cases involved the children of employees." Also, almost all of the children were "diagnosed as having adjustment or character disorders, problems that are either situational or behaviorally ingrained and for which, in many cases, there are equally effective out-patient treatments."[9]

This market is so lucrative that health care companies are trying to establish services whether or not they are needed. For example, the Tennessee Health Facilities Commission was recently flooded with applications from hospitals and health care companies wanting to establish inpatient psychiatric programs for children in Tennessee even though the state commissioner of mental health services indicated that the state was already "seriously overbedded with child and adolescent psychiatric beds."[10] In 1987, the Ohio Department of Mental Health received sixty-three applications for 2,112 new child and adolescent inpatient psychiatric beds. Despite intense lobbying on the part of many of the applicants, the director of the department gave the approval for only an additional 186 beds. The director's decision was based, in part, on an assessment of the mental health needs of children and youth in the state.[11] Now, many of the applicants have filed appeals to have their proposals reconsidered. Also, according to reports from departmental staff, the applicants have stepped up their lobbying efforts and are exerting pressure on the governor to intervene on their behalf.

For some hospitals, it's a matter of economic survival. They either have to move into providing these services—now commonly referred to as behavioral medicine—or close their doors.

The Center for the Study of Youth Policy estimates that inpatient psychiatric services for juveniles generated nearly $14 million in income for Minneapolis/St. Paul area hospitals in 1985. Table 7–1 shows just how expensive these services are, and they are becoming more costly each year.

A Look Inside the "Hidden" System

Finding out about the "hidden" system isn't easy. There are no comprehensive data on the number of juveniles being treated in inpatient psychiatric and chemical dependency units in private hospitals and in free-standing residential settings. What data exist are limited and are often difficult for researchers, health care policy analysts, and child advocates to obtain. The overwhelming majority

Table 7–1

JUVENILE INPATIENT PSYCHIATRIC AND CHEMICAL
DEPENDENCY TREATMENT, AVERAGE LENGTH OF
STAY AND CHARGE PER CASE, MINNEAPOLIS/ST.
PAUL METROPOLITAN AREA, 1978–85

Year	Chemical Dependency Treatment		Psychiatric Treatment	
	Average Length of Stay (days)	Average Charge per Case	Average Length of Stay (days)	Average Charge per Case
1978	24.7	$1,937	24.4	$2,434
1979	25.3	2,512	25.0	2,512
1980	27.3	2,446	27.8	3,299
1981	23.3	2,542	27.9	3,677
1982	24.7	2,938	27.4	3,856
1983	27.0	3,713	29.6	5,202
1984	28.2	4,589	28.9	5,675
1985	30.1	5,034	27.6	6,573

Source: Blue Cross and Blue Shield of Minnesota.
Note: Charges may or may not be reimbursed at 100 percent (state residents only).

of juveniles propelled into these programs are "voluntary" admissions—meaning that they do not go through the juvenile courts—and the services are largely paid for by third-party health care insurance and by parents. Comparatively little in the way of public funds is involved. More important, what goes on in the system takes place largely behind locked doors, some of which the "care givers" would just as soon not be made public.

What little data exist suggest that the "hidden" system is growing rapidly. Figures from the National Institute of Mental Health indicate that 16,735 adolescents were admitted to private psychiatric hospitals in 1980.[12] In 1985, the National Association of Private Psychiatric Hospitals estimated that that number had ballooned to 35,000.[13] These data reflect only a small part of the overall picture, because perhaps as few as 20 percent of all juvenile psychiatric admissions occur in hospitals that serve only psychiatric patients. For example, although 16,735 youth were admitted to private psychiatric hospitals in 1980, 48,185 children were admitted to units in general hospitals during the same year.[14] As indicated in table 7–2, the number and rate of juvenile admissions to inpatient

Table 7–2
JUVENILE INPATIENT PSYCHIATRIC ADMISSIONS AND PATIENT DAYS, MINNEAPOLIS/ST. PAUL METROPOLITAN AREA, 1977–1985

	Juvenile Psychiatric Admissions		
Year	Number	Rate per 100,000	Patient Days
1977	1,062	88	53,730
1979	1,623	142	68,949
1981	1,745	159	72,381
1983	2,031	184	76,899
1985	2,203	199	78,892

Source: Metropolitan Health Planning Board. *Mental Health Index*, Minneapolis, Minnesota, 1985

psychiatric units in the Minneapolis/St. Paul area hospitals more than doubled in eight years. Not one of these admissions was in a private psychiatric hospital.

In Illinois, one of the few states beginning to collect comprehensive data on hospitalized children, 2,985 youth were discharged from hospitals for psychiatric and drug or alcohol disorders during the first six months of fiscal year 1985–86. The number discharged increased to 3,604 during the last six months of the same fiscal year, an increase of approximately 21 percent.[15]

Data from the National Institute of Mental Health, and the Commission for Professional and Hospital Activities indicate that the majority of the juveniles placed in hospitals are not psychotic or hard-core cases of drug addiction or alcoholism. Nationally, about half the juveniles admitted to general hospitals for psychiatric diagnoses have "miscellaneous mental disorders" or "adjustment reactions and acute reactions to stress." More than 35 percent of the juveniles admitted to general hospitals under chemical diagnoses are there for nondependent use of drugs and alcohol.[16] Many of the cases are simply youth who have had a falling out with their parents and are rebellious. Some are the status offenders who used to be locked up in the juvenile justice system.

For example, Barbara, a 14-year-old girl, spent eighty-five days in an inpatient psychiatric unit. Her diagnosis was "adjustment reaction mixed with depression." She was admitted for "staying out all night without telling her mother and [because she got into] arguments over rules and conduct at home."[17]

Jodie was 17 when her parents admitted her to a psychiatric hospital in Los Angeles. She was put there because her parents were upset that she was dating a 31-year-old man. After Jodie had been dating this man for about seven months, and over the strong objections of her parents, she gave him $1,000 to invest for her. According to Jodie, her boyfriend has money of his own and does quite well with his investments in the stock market.

Jodie's medical record indicated that she was an A student and had been getting along well at home until she met her boyfriend. She was diagnosed as having an "adjustment reaction of adolescence with severe parental defiance and major errors in judgment." Jodie is now out of the hospital and in the process of suing the hospital and its staff for malpractice. Also, according to a mental health advocate in Los Angeles, Jodie received a $7,000 return on the money her boyfriend invested for her.[18]

Quality of Treatment

Many insurance companies and parents who pay from $200 to $600 a day or more for inpatient psychiatric and chemical dependency treatment for children think that they are paying for pretty good care. This is not always the case. For example, "one private psychiatric hospital [in Los Angeles County] served its new adolescent patients only a cheese sandwich and milk for each meal until they earned enough points to eat other items." Another private psychiatric hospital in the same community "conducted routine strip searches, where female adolescents had to squat, en masse, and were on occasion subjected to involuntary pelvic exams for contraband."[19] These practices were ended only after these hospitals were investigated by staff from the Los Angeles County Patients' Rights and Advocacy Services Program and were threatened with some type of official action.

Many of the programs use simplistic and punitive behavior modification regimes, similar to those once popular in juvenile training schools. There's a heavy reliance on the use of solitary confinement in places euphemistically referred to as "quiet" rooms, "time-out" rooms and "freedom" rooms, often for minor misbehavior. In some cases, children are not allowed to send or receive mail or have visitors, including their own parents. There have also been instances in which children were locked in their rooms until they agreed to "cooperate" with a therapist. Also, although many of the problems confronted by the youth incarcerated in these places are familycentered or involve other family members, very little work is done with families.

The Mental Health Unit of Saint Luke's Hospital in Duluth, Minnesota, uses an "adolescent code" system. It's an example of the primitive and rigid programming typically found in these places. The following are excerpts from an informational sheet given to young patients when they're first admitted that describes the program and what is expected of them:

> The code system is a program to help us learn about your behavior and allows you to earn privileges. You will be on a code where you can do what is expected of you and where staff can watch over you until we know you better. The staff and doctor will decide where you start. This will be decided when we know why you are here and what your behavior is like.
>
> A staff person will talk to you and tell you about the codes and what you need to do. They will answer any questions you have. Once a staff person has talked to you it is up to you to follow the rules and ask any questions if you are unsure of what to do.
>
> You can then work at going up the codes as you begin sharing about yourself, following the rules and being responsible for your behavior. Code raises will be up to the staff and your doctor and will be given only when you are following through with the program at the code you are on.
>
> You can also go down the codes. Some of the reasons could be: not following your code; out of control behavior; running or trying to run away; or, having drugs, weapons, or tobacco.[20]

All children placed in the program are required to prepare a written list of their problems and what they will do to correct them. They are also required to meet with a nurse every day to talk about their problems and concerns. If you don't "share" about yourself, you don't get more privileges. The youth placed on "code 1," the lowest level of the program, are housed in a closed or locked unit. They must wear hospital pajamas and cannot have any of their own belongings, including jewelry, or wear makeup. They aren't even allowed to leave their rooms except to participate in group treatment sessions. Youth who progress to "code 2" have essentially the same restrictions, except that they are allowed to leave their rooms more often and can leave the unit for tests with staff. They can also stay up a half-hour longer at night. It isn't until they graduate to "code 3" that the staff members begin to treat the youth with some decency by allowing them to wear their own clothes and use makeup if they so choose.[21]

Mary, a 14-year-old girl from California, thought that she was being taken to an outpatient therapy session. Instead, she was forcibly admitted to an inpatient hospital psychiatric unit. Since she was not aware she was to be hospitalized, she had not brought additional clothing with her. She was not allowed to use the phone, so she could not ask her parents to bring her extra clothes. Mary asked the staff to tell her parents about her predicament, but they failed to do so. As a result, Mary had to wash out and wear the same pair of underpants and wear the same dress every day. This lasted for a week until a mental health advocate discovered the situation and intervened on Mary's behalf.

Paul, a 17-year-old from a small town in Michigan, found himself in a locked psychiatric unit in a private hospital in Minneapolis. His case is another example of the abuses that are occurring under the guise of medical treatment. Paul comes from a single-parent family and had been having trouble getting along with his mother. He left the house on a couple of occasions and lived with friends. He dropped out of school and found work. When he decided to return home, his mother told him that the only route home was via a hospital stay in Minnesota.

Paul's mother had come into contact with the outreach program of a Minnesota hospital. As a result of those contacts, Paul's mother apparently became convinced that Paul had a chemical dependency problem, a problem Paul consistently denied. After less than a week in the chemical dependency unit, during which the hospital wasn't able to substantiate a diagnosis of chemical dependency, Paul was transferred to the hospital's locked psychiatric unit. The transfer was motivated, in part, by the fact that Paul didn't think he belonged on the chemical dependency unit and refused to participate in any of the activities there.

Shortly after Paul's transfer to the psychiatric unit, the staff imposed some restrictions on his behavior because of his "negative challenging attitude." Paul reacted by becoming hostile and threatened to "take on the staff." At that point he was placed in a "time-out" room, where he was kept overnight. Following his stay in the time-out room, he was grounded to his room, with no privileges whatsoever. The facility failed to follow its own policies of obtaining a physician's order for the seclusion or notifying the physician that the time-out lasted for more than an hour.

At the time of these incidents, Paul managed to contact the Legal Aid Society of Minneapolis. When Legal Aid lawyers first visited Paul, they found that there was no psychiatric or other diagnosis in Paul's chart, despite the fact that he had been hospitalized for several weeks. The hospital staff assured the attorneys that a diagnosis would be rendered before a bill was submitted to the insurance company. The hospital where Paul was confined was subsequently cited by the state health department for violations in the use of solitary confinement. Although the state health department investigation also substantiated the fact that Paul's transfer from the chemical dependency unit to the locked psychiatric unit was without any diagnoses of psychiatric problems, it found no violation, because the hospital claimed that the transfer was for "evaluation" purposes.

Does Hospitalization Work?

When people go into a hospital for medical treatment, it is not unusual for them to expect to get well or to be cured. Although hospital advertisements give the impression that their inpatient psychiatric and chemical dependency programs are effective, there's not one shred of credible scientific evidence to support any of these claims. For example, the findings from a study on children's mental health services conducted by the Office of Technology Assessment of the U.S. Congress indicated that "the effectiveness of psychiatric hospitalization for treating childhood mental disorders has not been studied systematically."[22] The researchers also found:

> Available studies do not clearly show which components of hospital treatment contribute to successful outcomes. Neither do they allow conclusions about whether children treated as hospital in-patients

would have been better, worse, or similar outcomes with non-hospital treatment.[23]

The same state of affairs exists with respect to inpatient chemical dependency treatment for children. There's a remarkable absence of solid research regarding the effectiveness of residential care as well as an absence of reliable criteria delineating which cases would be most suitable for such treatment. Researchers with the Rand Corporation recently completed an exhaustive study of what is known about the prevention and treatment of adolescent drug abuse. The Rand researchers found that "there is no consensus on the current state of drug abuse treatment"[24] and that "few if any treatments are backed up by persuasive scientific evidence."[25]

They also found that evaluating the effectiveness of such treatment is further complicated because:

- Many youth are in treatment involuntarily, having been brought in by parents or by authorities as a substitute for criminal sanctions. Their motivation is consequently suspect.
- Youth are often treated in unsuitable programs—usually, programs designed primarily for heroin addicts—whereas youth are rarely physically addicted to the drugs they abuse.
- While the consensus of researchers is that drug abuse in youth is best viewed as a problem of interpersonal relationships, the traditional treatments for drug abuse are based on theories that ascribe the problem to biological or psychological malfunctions."[26]

Discussion

Hospitals are rapidly becoming the new jails for middle-class and upper-middle-class kids. Using slick and often misleading advertising techniques, hospitals are seducing parents into hospitalizing their children. The children are usually committed for behavior problems that do not require hospitalization and for which there is little evidence that psychiatric intervention is appropriate or effective.

Hospitals are scurrying to get into the kid psychiatric and chemical dependency business because:

1. Status offenders can no longer be locked up in institutions in the juvenile justice system, and there is a lack of appropriate community-based alternatives for these youth and their families.

2. There is an excess of hospital beds because fewer people are going into hospitals for general medical and surgical care and because the average length of stay in hospitals has declined for those who do. Consequently, hospital administrators are looking for ways to fill their empty spaces and keep their facilities open.

3. Third-party health care insurance programs provide fiscal incentives that heavily favor inpatient over outpatient care. Also, children are particularly vulnerable to being confined in inpatient psychiatric and chemical dependency units, because they can be hospitalized under admissions criteria that are extremely vague and not scientifically grounded (for example, conduct disorder, adolescent adjustment reaction, emotional disturbance, chemical dependency).

There are children who are psychotic and who are a clear and substantial threat to themselves and others. Also, there are youth who are hard-core drug addicts and alcoholics. These youth need to be hospitalized and provided with the best professional care possible. However, it is clear that these youth represent a very small proportion of the ones who end up in hospital inpatient and psychiatric chemical dependency units. This raises a number of significant issues that need to be addressed by policymakers, health care experts, insurance carriers, child advocates, legal experts, health care professionals, health care professional associations, public interest groups, and parents. For example:

1. The overwhelming majority of children being locked up in hospital psychiatric and chemical dependency units are being admitted under the guise of receiving medical treatment. Because most of them are essentially admitted for behavioral and family-related problems, not for serious disorders requiring hospitalization, these youth are essentially being incarcerated without the benefit of due process. Moreover, they are in a legal "twilight zone." They are not involuntary patients, because they have not been committed by the courts. They are also not voluntary patients, because they cannot

walk out of a program if they so choose. Sharon's case is illustrative of this problem.

Sharon is 15 years old and has run away from home on numerous occasions. She has experimented with marijuana but has never used hard drugs. She runs away because her father is a heavy drinker, particularly when he's under pressure at work. When he drinks too much, he becomes violent and verbally and physically abuses Sharon and her mother. He has also made sexual advances toward Sharon.

Sharon's parents, upon the advice of a school counselor, admitted her to a locked psychiatric unit in a private hospital. The hospital's records indicate that she was diagnosed as having an adolescent adjustment problem and that she was pre-chemically dependent.

2. Some potentially adverse long-term implications of hospitalizing children for psychiatric and chemical dependency treatment have to be carefully explored. For instance, children who are hospitalized for psychiatric and drug and alcohol treatment might find that they are discriminated against by potential employers; that they may encounter difficulties if they choose to run for public office, adopt a child, or purchase insurance; or that they may be excluded from entering certain occupations. Roy and his wife were refused a home mortgage loan when the bank they applied to found him to be an "unacceptable risk" because he had spent several months in an inpatient chemical dependency unit in a private hospital when he was 16 years old.

3. Third-party health care insurance programs and mandatory health care insurance laws that have fiscal incentives favoring inpatient over outpatient care need to be reformed. They need to be reformed along the lines of encouraging the development and use of a wider variety of outpatient services and discouraging the use of hospital-based care. This is particularly important in light of the mounting evidence that appropriate outpatient care is as effective as inpatient treatment for many cases and much less costly. For example, the findings from a recent study comparing the effectiveness of intensive home-based services as an alternative to the placement of seriously emotionally disturbed adolescents in group homes and residential treatment centers indicate that many of these more costly and restrictive placements can be prevented.[27] Also, the

excessive use of hospital-based treatment must be curtailed because it is contributing to the spiraling costs of health care generally.

4. State lawmakers should enact legislation requiring that constitutional and humane programmatic standards be developed for the operation of inpatient psychiatric and chemical dependency units in hospitals and free-standing residential facilities. They should also require that these institutions be independently monitored on a regular basis.

5. State policymakers should reexamine their existing civil commitment statues regarding children and, where necessary, update these laws to ensure that they provide youth with adequate due process protections without prohibiting access to appropriate treatment when needed. This is particularly important in light of the growing evidence that older adolescents are as capable of making competent decisions, even about their own medical treatment, as adults.[28]

Notes

1. U.S. Congress, House (1985), p. 48.
2. Fair Oakes Hospital (1987).
3. Golden Valley Health Center (1987).
4. Kamber (1987).
5. *Wall Street Journal* (1985).
6. *Akron Beacon Journal* (1987), p. 1.
7. Polich et al. (1984), p. xii.
8. *New York Times* (1986), p. 30.
9. Blackburn (1986), p. 41.
10. Sivley (1986).
11. Ohio Department of Mental Health (1987).
12. Millazzo-Sayre et al. (1986).
13. Jackson-Beeck, Schwartz, and Rutherford (1987); p. 7.
14. Millazzo-Sayre et al. (1986), p. 12.
15. Illinois Health Care Cost Containment Council (1987), p. 1.
16. Commission for Professional and Hospital Activities (1985), pp. 63–74.
17. Flygare (1986), p. 39.
18. Lurie (1987).
19. Lurie (1986).
20. Saint Luke's Hospital (1986).
21. Ibid.
22. U.S. Congress, Office of Technology Assessment (1986), p. 3.
23. Ibid., pp. 118–19.

24. Polich et al. (1984), p. 100.
25. Ibid., p. 101.
26. Ibid., p. 114.
27. AuClaire and Schwartz (1986).
28. Melton and Pilner (1986).

References

Akron Beacon Journal. 4 October 1987. "The Fight for Mental-Health Profits."

AuClaire, P., and Schwartz, I. M. 1986. *An Evaluation of the Effectiveness of Intensive Home-Based Services as an Alternative to Placement for Adolescents and Their Families.* Minneapolis: University of Minnesota, Hubert H. Humphrey Institute of Public Affairs.

Blackburn, C. 1986. "Employee Assistance Programs: Getting a Handle on Costs and Quality." *Pace* 14 (2): 41.

Commission for Professional and Hospital Activities (CPHA). 1985. *Length of Stay by Diagnosis, U.S.* Ann Arbor, Mich.: CPHA.

Fair Oaks Hospital. 1987. Advertisement. *Fort Lauderdale News/Sun Sentinel.*

Flygare, S. 1986. "Civil Commitment of Juveniles: Available Facilities and Funds." In *Placing Kids in Treatment: Who Has What Rights?* St. Paul, Minn.: Hamline University, Advanced Legal Education.

Golden Valley Health Center. 13 January 1987. Advertisement. *Minneapolis Star and Tribune,* p. 4B.

Illinois Health Care Cost Containment Council. November 1987. *Psychiatric Inpatient Stays, Counts and Average Length of Stay by Patient-Age and Discharge Date.* Report No. 4. Unpublished document.

Jackson-Beeck, M.; Schwartz, I.M.; and Rutherford, A. 1987. *Trends and Issues in Juvenile Confinement for Psychiatric and Chemical Dependency Treatment in the U.S., England, and Wales.* Minneapolis: University of Minnesota, Center for the Study of Youth Policy.

Kamber, S. 3 February 1987. Letter to Ira M. Schwartz.

Lurie, B.D. 15 October 1987. Letter to Ira M. Schwartz.

Lurie, B.D. 18 July 1986. Letter to Ira M. Schwartz.

Melton, G.B., and Pilner, A.J. 1986. "Adolescent Abortion: A Psychology Analysis, I." In *Adolescent Abortion,* ed. G.B. Melton. Lincoln: University of Nebraska Press.

Millazzo-Sayre, L.J.; Benson, P.R.; Rosenthal, M.J.; and Manderscheid, R.W. 1986. *Use of In-patient Psychiatric Facilities by Children and Youth Under 18, United States, 1980.* Statistical Note No. 175. Rockville, Md.: National Institute of Mental Health.

New York Times. 7 October 1986. "Mental Health Costs Soaring."

Polich, J.M.; Ellickson, P.L.; Reuter, P.; and Kahan, J.P. 1984. *Strategies for Controlling Adolescent Drug Use.* Santa Monica, Calif.: Rand Corporation.

Saint Luke's Hospital, Mental Health Unit. 1986. "Adolescent Code." Duluth, Minn. (photocopy).

Sivley, R.D. 18 August 1986. Letter to Robert C. Wortman.

U.S. Congress, House, Select Committee on Children, Youth and Families. 1985. *Emerging Trends in Mental Health Care for Adolescents*. 99th Cong., 1st sess.

U.S. Congress, Office of Technology Assessment. December 1986. *Children's Mental Health Problems and Services: A Background Paper*. Washington, D.C.: U.S. Government Printing Office.

Wall Street Journal. 19 June 1985.

8

The Juvenile Court

I N 1999, the juvenile court will be 100 years old. Although some were skeptical about the creation of this special court for children, and although the court has had a turbulent history and is still not without its critics, the juvenile court is a firmly entrenched social institution that enjoys broad-based support. Although it appears that the juvenile court is not in any immediate danger of disappearing from the juvenile justice landscape, there is clear and convincing evidence that many of the youth who come into contact with the court for delinquency and status offense behavior receive second-rate justice.

"You're Entitled to an Attorney if You Can't Afford One, but . . ."

In 1977, ten years after the *Gault* decision, I headed up a study of the juvenile court services system in Wisconsin. The study was being conducted by the John Howard Association, and I was the association's executive director at the time. One of the consultants who worked on the study spent a lot of time observing juvenile court hearings and interviewing judges. One evening, he told me that he had observed some court hearings that were particularly interesting. He said that the judge had been very careful in explaining and making sure that all of the juveniles who appeared before him understood their rights. However, when children appeared before him who could not afford to hire an attorney, the judge would lean across his desk, look them squarely in the eye, and tell them that although they had the right to an attorney at public expense, he would take the fact that they wanted a court-appointed attorney into account if they were found guilty. The implication was that they might receive a more severe sanction if they were found guilty and the county had to pay for the cost of their representation. It was not surprising that the overwhelming majority of juveniles who appeared before this particular judge and couldn't afford a lawyer waived their right to counsel. Some people will claim that this is a rare and isolated example. As we shall see, there is reason to believe that such practices are far more common than people realize.

The History of the Juvenile Court

The juvenile court had its beginnings in the Progressive movement during the late 1800s and early 1900s. The rapid industrialization and urbanization of America, coupled with the large influx of immigrants from southern and eastern Europe at the turn of the century, contributed to the problems of poverty, inadequate housing, disease, and the economic exploitation of children. These problems prompted action on the part of social and political reformers. The reformers were also concerned about the ways in which children who came to the attention of the authorities were dealt with. For example, they were outraged because juvenile law violators were treated no differently than adult criminals. These children were often subjected to harsh punishments and were confined in jails and prisons with adult offenders. This period also witnessed growing interest in the scientific approach to the amelioration of social problems and in the belief that the social sciences would provide answers to these problems. This influenced reformers to advocate for nonpunitive measures and an emphasis on individualized diagnosis and treatment of children based on the medical model, a concept more popularly known as the "rehabilitative ideal."

The result was the creation of a special court in which children were denied due process and adversarial proceedings in exchange for informal and confidential hearings and dispositions based on what was felt to be in the "best interests of the child." It was a court in which "the distinctions between dependent, neglected and delinquent children were less important than their common need for state supervision in the manner of a wise and devoted parent."[1]

The first juvenile court was created in Cook County (Chicago),

Illinois, in 1899. The concept spread quickly throughout the country, and by 1917, "all but three states created special courts for children."[2] Although there are conflicting reports about whether the creation of the juvenile court was motivated entirely by benevolent concerns, the establishment of a separate court for children is generally viewed as one of the most important advances in the welfare of children in the history of our country.

The creators of the juvenile court envisioned that this special court for children would be less like a court and more like a social welfare agency. Children who were brought to the attention of the juvenile court were to be helped rather than punished. There was to be less concern with determining guilt or innocence and more emphasis on identifying the causes of a child's misbehavior and prescribing individualized treatment. As stated earlier, children were not to be subjected "to the rigors of formal criminal trials" but were to be handled informally.[3] In exchange for this informality, they were denied the rights and procedural safeguards accorded to adults.

This philosophy remained intact for nearly seventy years. Some legal scholars and child advocates questioned the wisdom of this philosophy; they were concerned about abuses that occurred within this informal and benevolent system. However, the skeptics were few compared to the growing legion of supporters for this concept. Then, beginning in 1966, abuses in the system were brought to the attention of the U.S. Supreme Court, which, in a series of decisions, "held that juveniles are entitled to a broad range of procedural protections previously denied them."[4]

For example, in *Kent v. United States*, the court was confronted with the issue of the process by which a juvenile court waives a young person to be tried in the adult courts. In examining this case, the Court found:

> There is evidence, in fact, that there may be grounds for concern that the child receives the worst of both worlds: that he gets neither the protections accorded to adults nor the solicitous care and regenerative treatment postulated for children.[5]

The Court held that a "juvenile must be given a formal hearing on the 'critically important' issue of whether a juvenile court should try the child or waive jurisdiction and transfer the case to an adult criminal court."[6] The Court also held that "if a juvenile court does decide to waive jurisdiction, it must provide a written statement of reasons for the decision sufficient to enable meaningful appellate review."[7]

In *In re Gault*, the Court wrestled with questions regarding which due process protections apply "to the proceedings by which a determination is made as to whether a juvenile is a 'delinquent' as a result of alleged misconduct on his part, with the consequence that he may be committed to a state institution."[8] After carefully reviewing the facts in this case, the Court reiterated that "due process of law is the primary and indispensable foundation of individualized freedom"[9] and noted that the "condition of being a boy does not justify a kangaroo court."[10] The Court held that

> (1) the child and his parents must be given adequate and timely notice of charges against the child so that they will have reasonable opportunity to prepare for the hearing; (2) the child and his parents must be advised of the child's right to be represented by counsel and if they are unable to afford counsel, that counsel will be appointed; (3) the privilege against self-incrimination is applicable to juvenile proceedings; and (4) the child has a right to confront and cross-examine witnesses against him.[11]

Child advocates, legal scholars, and reformers applauded these decisions and predicted that they would revolutionize the juvenile court. Some people remained skeptical. Events in the intervening years since these landmark U.S. Supreme Court decisions suggest that the skeptics had good reason to be concerned.

Justice for Children: An Elusive Goal

Few will argue with the assertion that the U.S. Supreme Court's intervention in juvenile justice has been constructive. What is subject to question is the extent to which the Court's decisions have actually improved justice for children. This is an important question, because the kangaroo court the Supreme Court referred to in *In re Gault* still exists in some parts of this country. For example, in Arkansas, the county courts have traditionally had responsibility for juvenile court matters. In January 1987, the Arkansas Supreme

Court ruled that "the exercise of exclusive jurisdiction over juveniles is not a permissible function of the county courts under the Arkansas Constitution."[12] The Arkansas Supreme Court found that "county courts do not . . . possess the same judicial safeguards as other state courts" and that they "have been unable to ensure the proper disposition of juvenile delinquency cases."[13]

The Arkansas Supreme Court based its findings, in part, on the results of a study conducted by the Arkansas Advocates for Children and Families. The study consisted of observations of 492 juvenile cases in forty-six county courts in Arkansas in 1983. The researchers found:

1. In at least 15 percent of the cases, juveniles who appeared for their adjudicatory hearing without an attorney were not advised of their right to counsel.

2. The right to remain silent . . . was not announced at approximately 30 percent of the plea and adjudication hearings observed. . . . [Also,] juveniles were required to testify at more than one-third of the adjudication hearings.

3. Prosecutors . . . presented the state's case only about 20 percent of the time while probation officers—persons in whom the juveniles were expected to place their confidence—presented the state's case against juveniles twice as often. Referees and county judges—the impartial officers of the court—also presented the case against the juveniles at some hearings.

4. Defense attorneys . . . were not present at about two out of three hearings. Even some juveniles sentenced to the training school were not represented by an attorney.

5. The ramifications of entering a plea of guilty were not explained to the juvenile at about three out of ten plea hearings.

6. Neither the complainant nor the complainant's witnesses were present at close to 40 percent of the judicial hearings at which the defense normally should be able to confront its accuser. Most witnesses for the prosecution were placed under oath and the defense given an opportunity to question them, but such was not the case at more than one-fourth of the hearings.[14]

The Arkansas study is one of the few of its kind. Although it portrays a sad state of affairs for the children who come before the courts in Arkansas, its findings are somewhat consistent with, though not as dismal as, the observations in and reports from some other states. For example, despite the Supreme Court's ruling in *In re Gault* that children have a right to counsel when faced with the possibility that they may be deprived of their liberty, many young people never see a lawyer or waive their right to counsel, often at the encouragement of a judge, a probation officer, or someone else serving in an official capacity.

Feld recently completed a study of juvenile representation in six states and in one large city: California, Minnesota, Nebraska, New York, North Dakota, Pennsylvania, and Philadelphia. He found that approximately half of the juveniles who appeared before the courts for delinquency and status offense matters in three of the states (Minnesota, Nebraska, and North Dakota) were not represented by counsel. Moreover, he found that many of the youth who were placed out of their homes in these states did not have lawyers.[15]

A Florida Center for Children and Youth study of Florida's compliance with the Juvenile Justice and Delinquency Prevention Act of 1974 indicated that juvenile justice officials in Florida reported that status offenders were "seldom" or "never" represented by counsel and that only about a third of the status offenders who had violated a court order and were held in contempt of court had attorneys. More alarming was the fact that many of the respondents, particularly judges and prosecutors, indicated that they didn't feel that status offenders were entitled to representation, even though Florida statutes require that youth have access to counsel if they are in danger of being removed from their homes.[16]

A study by the legislature in Minnesota indicated that more than half of the juveniles who appeared before the courts for delinquency and status offense cases were not represented by counsel at either the adjudicatory or dispositional stage. More than 25 percent of the youth committed to training schools were not represented by an attorney at their dispositional hearings.[17] Also, as indicated in table 8–1, there are enormous variations among Minnesota's eighty-seven counties with respect to juveniles being represented by counsel. In Hennepin County—the largest county in the state, which includes the city of Minneapolis and its suburbs—only 44 percent of the youth appearing before the juvenile courts were represented at the adjudicatory stage, and only 48 percent had the benefit of counsel at

Table 8–1
LEGAL REPRESENTATION OF JUVENILES IN STATUS
AND DELINQUENCY CASES, MINNESOTA, 1984

County	Legal Representation at Adjudicatory Stage			Legal Representation at Dispositional Stage		
	No. of Cases	No. Rep.	Percent Rep.	No. of Cases	No. Rep.	Percent Rep.
Aitkin	31	7	23	29	6	21
Anoka	557	557	100	629	628	100
Becker	116	40	35	116	40	35
Beltrami	164	36	22	175	39	22
Bentein	72	24	33	73	25	34
Bigstone	19	4	21	5	2	40
Blue Earth	158	42	27	155	41	26
Brown	116	22	19	105	21	20
Carlton	209	77	37	217	80	37
Carver	202	51	25	211	60	28
Cass	135	59	44	102	50	49
Chippewa	28	6	21	29	8	28
Chisago	73	36	49	49	24	49
Clay	196	52	27	200	56	28
Clearwater	39	14	36	33	14	42
Cook	17	3	18	10	3	30
Cottonwood	36	7	19	28	6	21
Crow Wing	147	16	11	82	15	18
Dakota	539	538	100	242	241	100
Dodge	40	12	30	36	11	31
Douglas	104	27	26	103	25	24
Fairbault	36	4	11	32	5	16
Fillmore	39	18	46	39	18	46
Freeborn	115	25	22	86	22	26
Goodhue	108	27	25	98	26	27
Grant	27	0	0	15	0	0
Hennepin	4,513	1,997	44	4,179	2,022	48
Houston	50	10	20	47	10	21
Hubbard	71	43	61	49	30	61
Isanti	102	40	39	61	33	54
Itasca	254	49	19	253	56	22
Jackson	40	7	18	20	11	55
Kanabec	17	16	94	11	11	100
Kandiyohi	106	27	26	103	25	24
Kittson	27	5	19	22	4	18
Loochiching	42	2	5	35	1	3
Lac Qui Poule	18	5	28	6	2	33
Lake	9	5	56	1	0	0
Lake of Woods	23	4	17	22	2	9
LeSeur	65	37	57	68	42	62
Lincoln	5	1	20	5	1	20
Lyon	22	8	36	12	5	42
Mcleod	71	10	14	72	13	18
Mahnomen	30	11	37	26	16	62
Marshall	43	9	21	43	9	21

Table 8–1 continued

LEGAL REPRESENTATION OF JUVENILES IN STATUS AND DELINQUENCY CASES, MINNESOTA, 1984

County	Legal Representation at Adjudicatory Stage			Legal Representation at Dispositional Stage		
	No. of Cases	No. Rep.	Percent Rep.	No. of Cases	No. Rep.	Percent Rep.
Martin	22	14	64	20	17	85
Meeker	55	15	27	53	17	32
Mille Lacs	91	25	27	86	25	29
Morrison	126	15	12	114	14	12
Mower	139	22	16	58	18	31
Murray	46	13	28	37	11	30
Nicollet	115	17	15	127	23	18
Nobles	39	8	21	41	12	29
Norman	17	9	53	15	9	60
Olmsted	166	56	34	171	73	43
Ottertail	228	52	23	235	60	26
Pennington	51	5	10	17	3	18
Pine	52	49	94	31	27	87
Pipestone	31	14	45	31	14	45
Polk	121	29	24	120	35	29
Pope	26	1	4	24	1	4
Ramsey	2,052	1,716	84	2,756	864	31
Red Lake	3	1	33	3	1	33
Redwood	92	15	16	56	8	14
Renville	46	5	11	13	4	31
Rice	136	36	27	133	41	31
Rock	5	0	0	5	0	0
Roseau	22	5	23	22	5	23
St. Louis	585	310	53	573	281	49
Scott	183	49	27	185	55	30
Sherburne	115	19	17	46	11	24
Sibley	29	10	35	8	5	63
Stearns	204	36	18	225	35	16
Steele	115	14	12	118	13	11
Stevens	20	1	5	20	1	5
Swift	55	26	47	18	15	83
Todd	68	12	18	70	14	20
Traverse	22	1	5	26	2	8
Wabasha	57	8	14	18	8	44
Wadena	36	13	36	36	12	33
Waseca	47	11	23	48	14	29
Washington	355	297	84	358	304	85
Watonwan	70	11	16	27	7	26
Wilkin	109	43	39	113	45	40
Winona	237	9	4	227	8	4
Wright	321	33	10	337	24	7
Yellow Medicine	15	3	20	6	3	50
Totals	15,155	7,018	46	14,561	5,898	41

Source: Criminal Justice Statistical Analysis Center, State Planning Agency, St. Paul, Minnesota.

the dispositional stage. In Ramsey County—the second largest county in the state, which includes the city of St. Paul and its suburbs—84 percent of the juveniles were represented by counsel at their adjudicatory hearings, but less than one-third were represented at the dispositional stage.

For the past several years, child advocates, public interest groups, the Minnesota state juvenile justice advisory committee, and some juvenile justice and child welfare professionals have been trying to get the Minnesota legislature to modernize the state's juvenile justice, child welfare, and juvenile civil commitment statutes. They have had only limited success.

One of the proposed reforms that encounters some of the stiffest opposition is a proposal for an unwaivable right to counsel for children accused of crimes. Many judges, law enforcement officials, probation workers, and school social workers argue that providing every child with an attorney will only "slow down the process" and will delay getting children the "help" they need. Some argue that it would be too expensive; others think it's a bad idea because some youth who have committed crimes might "get off."

The differing opinions about whether juveniles should have access to representation are interesting and revealing. They are also opinions that are not confined to the state of Minnesota. In fact, my travels around the country lead me to believe that there is far from a consensus on this issue in many jurisdictions. More important, it seems to me that the debate on this topic is symptomatic of a much larger and more fundamental problem. The problem is that there is something wrong with the juvenile court.

There are also questions about the quality of representation when it is provided. A two-year study of the Law Guardian Program in New York State found that many of the attorneys representing children in jurisdictions outside New York City have not been adequately trained to represent juveniles, are unfamiliar with relevant changes in legislation and case law pertaining to children, and are often inadequately prepared to represent their clients.[18] The overall conclusion from the study was

All the data point to excessive inadequacies in the general level of representation according to children, regardless of whether they are involved in delinquency type proceedings, or, as is increasingly the case, child protective proceedings and those related to out-of-home placements.[19]

The Juvenile Court as an Administrator of Services

Judge Luke Quinn often tells an interesting story about his experiences when he was first elected to the bench in Genessee County (Flint), Michigan. He mentions that he had no idea that when he became a judge he would also become a "jailer." In addition to his duties on the bench, Quinn discovered that he was responsible for the management of a seventy-two-bed juvenile detention center—a responsibility that he says he wasn't elected to perform, didn't feel particularly well qualified to do, and, more important, didn't even feel should be a responsibility of the courts. Quinn maintains that it was a conflict of interest for him to act as a judge and try to be impartial and make independent decisions in cases involving youth who appeared before him who had been confined in a detention center he administered. He found it awkward to sit in judgment on cases that included reports about youth submitted by his own detention staff.

Judge Quinn's story highlights another source of controversy surrounding the juvenile courts. This controversy centers on the problems and potential conflicts of interest when the court serves both as an impartial trier of facts and as an administrator of youth detention and correctional services. In many jurisdictions, the juvenile courts are responsible for the administration of juvenile detention centers, juvenile probation programs, youth correctional facilities, and other social service programs. As a publication from the Academy for Contemporary Problems noted:

> The possibility of conflicts of interest becomes evident when a judge is required to decide whether a detention decision was properly made, the conditions in a detention facility are violative of constitutional rights, or probation or intake policies are legal, while retaining responsibility for the administration of these same programs or facilities.[20]

Moreover, there is some evidence that juvenile courts that control probation, detention, and other youth correctional programs are less likely to be due process–oriented. In a study examining the performance of various juvenile courts, staff researchers from the National Center for State Courts found that "attorneys, both defense and prosecution, play a greater role in due process courts."[21] In courts where probation, detention, and related services are administered by an agency in the executive branch of government, children are more likely to be represented by counsel. In contrast, in jurisdictions where the juvenile courts administratively control such services, children are likely to have counsel only if they are accused of serious offenses or if there is a possibility of a disposition resulting in incarceration.[22]

Restructuring the Juvenile Court

The original concept of the juvenile court was an interesting idea that, to my mind, was well worth experimenting with. Few will argue with the assertion that the juvenile court movement has played an important role in developing and improving the quality of services for children and that it has had a major impact on policies related to children and families at the federal, state, and local levels. However, despite the important role that the court has played, the U.S. Supreme Court acknowledged in 1971 that the "fond and idealistic hopes of the juvenile court proponents and early reformers of three generations ago have not been realized."[23] It's time to recognize that those "fond and idealistic hopes" will never be realized.

Events of the past ninety years have taught us that the juvenile court's underlying assumptions were faulty, particularly as they relate to delinquency matters, that the expectations for it were unreasonable, and that it was saddled with a number of unresolvable internal inconsistencies. The informality and confidentiality of juvenile court proceedings and the broad discretion given to judges and other professionals working in the court contributed to widespread abuses—abuses that continue despite intervention by the U.S. Supreme Court. The situation is tantamount to sacrificing the civil liberties of children in exchange for "good intentions." The social sciences have proved to be remarkably incapable of delivering the accurate diagnostic and prescriptive treatment protocols that were envisioned. Moreover, the prospects for doing so in the foreseeable future are not very promising.

The juvenile court is burdened with the responsibility for making decisions that are in the "best interests of the child" while, at the same time, making decisions that will protect the public. The court is supposed to both treat and punish juvenile law violators, hardly compatible functions. "The decades since *Gault* have witnessed a substantial procedural convergence between juvenile courts and adult criminal courts."[24] However:

> Despite the criminalization of the juvenile court, it remains nearly as true today as two decades ago that "the child receives the worst of both worlds: that [the child] gets neither the protections accorded adults nor the solicitous care and regenerative treatment postulated for children." Most state juvenile codes provide neither special procedural safeguards to protect juveniles from the consequences of their own immaturity nor the full panoply of adult criminal procedural safeguards to protect them from punitive state intervention.[25]

Some people argue that the problems with the juvenile court are so severe and deep-rooted that it should be abolished. They maintain that the juvenile court cannot be reformed and that children will never be treated justly and fairly so long as it continues to exist. For example, Feld recently commented that "the juvenile court has demonstrated a remarkable ability to deflect, co-opt, and absorb ameliorative reform virtually without institutional change."[26]

I believe that the juvenile court may still prove to be a viable option. For this to happen, however, I feel that the juvenile court and our approaches to providing justice for children need to be restructured. The changes that need to be made should, at a minimum, conform with the following principles. First, we must acknowledge that "the court's primary purpose is to administer justice."[27]

Second, juveniles should have the same due process and procedural safeguards accorded to adults, with one exception: Juveniles should have a nonwaivable right to counsel:

> The high rate of waiver of counsel . . . is an indictment of the entire juvenile adjudicative apparatus because the effective assistance of counsel is the necessary prerequisite to the invocation of every other procedural safeguard.[28]

Nonwaivable right to counsel is also important because of the research indicating that "younger juveniles as a class do not understand the nature and significance of their Miranda rights to remain silent and to counsel. Consequently, their waiver of these rights cannot be considered intelligently, knowingly, and voluntarily made."[29] The U.S. Supreme Court ruled that adult defendants have a right to self-representation.[30] Providing juveniles with a nonwaivable right to counsel means that young people will actually have less freedom in this area than adults. However, this does not appear to be unreasonable, because one can hardly expect young people to be able to represent themselves competently when they don't understand the implications and full significance of their right to waive counsel. Some people will argue that the decision for nonwaivable right to counsel should be made on a case-by-case basis. Although this argument has some merit, so many children would qualify for mandatory representation that it would be impractical to implement such a procedure.

Third, delinquency proceedings should be open to the public and the media. Delinquency proceedings are conducted behind closed doors. This is done, presumably, to maintain confidentiality and to protect juveniles from being stigmatized and labeled by the community. In reality, these private proceedings have done little more than keep the public and the media from being able to monitor and scrutinize what really goes on in juvenile court. In 1986, the Minnesota legislature opened up delinquency hearings for 16- and 17-year-olds accused of committing felonies. The opponents of this reform measure predicted that it would have dire consequences for the youth involved. To date, there is no evidence that this change in the law has had any significant adverse impact.

Fourth, there should be mandatory rotation of juvenile court judges. The American Bar Association Standards of Juvenile Judicial Administration recommended assignment "for a period of one year, with renewal for no longer than two years."[31] This is a reasonable standard to follow, because it takes into account the need for stability while eliminating "one of the most pressing problems present in many juvenile courts—the formation of 'one man (or one woman) empires.'" The danger in the "one man (or one woman) empire" is that it often "results in a court that may be operated in a paternalistic manner with the legal safeguards of due process substantially ignored."[32]

Fifth, juvenile courts should not administer probation, detention, or related youth corrections and social service programs. In those jurisdictions where the courts do administer these services, policy-makers should move to have them transferred to an appropriate agency within the executive branch of government. However, the juvenile courts should have the capability and resources to monitor dispositions in order to ensure that they are being carried out and implemented properly.

Sixth, the juvenile courts should concentrate their resources on the cases involving serious delinquency. More than half of the juvenile justice cases referred to the juvenile courts each year are for status offenses and minor and petty crimes.[33] These cases consume a substantial amount of juvenile court time and resources, and they can be handled more effectively in other ways. More specifically, status offense cases should be removed from the jurisdiction of the juvenile courts. They should be handled by voluntary social and family service agencies, programs for runaway youth, mediation services, and the like. When appropriate, officials should intervene under existing state dependency and neglect statutes in order to protect those youth whose immediate health and welfare may be in real danger. We need to recognize that many children run away from intolerable home situations, particularly situations that involve physical and sexual abuse. It makes absolutely no sense to treat children who have the good sense to escape from an intolerable home situation the same way we treat juvenile criminals. Also, to the extent possible, the cases involving minor and petty crimes should be handled outside the court system. Expanded use of restitution, fines, and community service would be appropriate for many of these cases.

Seventh, the juvenile court should be a part of or a division within a state's general trial court, not a separate court. Also, there should be court administrative rules mandating rotation of judges. The rules should be modeled after the standards for a judicial rotation system recommended by the Institute for Judicial Administration/American Bar Association. These recommendations will help to raise the stature of the juvenile court and help to ensure that the most competent and well-qualified judges serve on the juvenile bench.

The juvenile court is still commonly referred to as the "kiddie court." Many judges, particularly the most able and well-respected ones, view assignment to the juvenile court as "punishment"—

something to be avoided. As a result, too many judges who are elected or assigned to the juvenile court bench are either incompetent or ill suited for the job.

For example, the circuit court in this one particular state does not have a rotation system. Judge X has been on the juvenile court bench for eight consecutive years. Judge X is considered to be inept. The chief judge won't reassign him to work in any of the other divisions of the court (for example, civil or criminal) because his is afraid that Judge X will be an embarrassment and that the chief judge might be put in the position of having to take disciplinary action. As a result, the chief judge "hides" Judge X in the juvenile court, where it is felt he can do the least amount of "damage."

The process of using referees as substitute judges in juvenile court should be eliminated or the role of the referee curtailed to nonadjudicatory matters.

Like so many other resources in the juvenile justice system, many courts do not have adequate judicial resources. Rather than providing fully qualified judges, referees are substituted. The referee appointment process is generally a patronage system and, in many cases, the job is held part time. This results in the appointment of less than qualified persons who are not fully attentive to the needs of the court.

If referees are needed to shore up the shortage of judges, why not use them in civil or probate courts to handle procedural matters and other matters that do not affect the lives of children and families? We profess the importance of the juvenile court, so why not assign it sufficient *judicial* resources?

Implementing this recommendation would help to dispel the second-class status of the juvenile court.

The foregoing principles inevitably lead to the question of whether the juvenile court should retain jurisdiction over delinquency matters or whether these matters should be handled by the adult criminal courts. It is clear that "when juvenile cases are moved into the adult criminal court system . . . they immediately are granted the full range of rights to due process and equal protection of law."[34] This may well be another option for policymakers to explore, but I have some reservations about it. In many jurisdictions, the adult criminal courts, particularly the misdemeanor courts, are seriously overcrowded. They couldn't absorb juvenile cases without added resources. Also, if juvenile cases were transferred to the adult criminal courts, it would be essential to keep the existing system of youth detention and corrections intact. Juveniles detained on a predispositional status should be confined in detention centers. When appropriate, they should be committed to small, high-security youth correctional facilities and other juvenile correctional programs. Juveniles should not be confined in adult jails or prisons.

Discussion

Since its creation in 1899, the juvenile court has become a permanent fixture on the juvenile justice and child welfare landscape. The juvenile courts typically have broad jurisdiction and discretion over dependency and neglect, child physical and sexual abuse, delinquency, and child custody matters. The juvenile court's ninety-year history in handling delinquency cases reveals that it is a highly idiosyncratic institution that is unable to guarantee that children receive adequate due process and procedural protections. In fact, there is evidence that what rights children do have are routinely disregarded or violated in many jurisdictions. I believe that it is time to recognize that due process and equality in justice are in the best interests of children. The best way to ensure that children receive justice is to respect their autonomy and dignity and provide them with the same rights as other citizens. If this can be accomplished within the existing juvenile court structure, all the better. If not, then it would be advisable to eliminate the juvenile court's jurisdiction over delinquency cases and have them handled in the adult criminal courts.

Notes

1. Ryerson (1978), p. 42.
2. Wadlington, Whitebread, and Davis (1983), p. 198.
3. Piersma et al (1977), p. 13.
4. Ibid.
5. *Kent v. United States* (1966), p. 556.
6. Piersma et al. (1977), p. 13.
7. Ibid., p. 14.
8. *In re Gault* (1967), p. 13.
9. Ibid., p. 20.
10. Ibid., p. 28.

11. Piersma et al. (1977), p. 14.
12. *Debra Lynn Walker v. Arkansas Department of Human Resources* (1987), p. 1.
13. Ibid., p. 7.
14. Arkansas Advocates for Children and Families (1983), pp. 1–2.
15. Feld (1987), p. 30.
16. Florida Center for Children and Youth (1988), pp. 63–64.
17. Fine (1983), p. 43.
18. Knitzer and Sobie (1984), pp. 6–9.
19. Ibid., p. 13.
20. Academy for Contemporary Problems (1981), p. 466.
21. Ito (1984), p. xxiii.
22. Ibid., pp. xv–xvi.
23. *McKeiver v. Pennsylvania* (1971), pp. 543–44.
24. Feld (1987), p. 529.
25. Ibid., pp. 529–30.
26. Feld (1984), p. 276.
27. Melton (1986), p. 4.
28. Feld (1984), p. 270.
29. Grisso (1980), p. 1166.
30. *Faretta v. California* (1974).
31. American Bar Association (1980), p. 19.
32. Ibid., p. 20.
33. Snyder, Hutzler, and Finnegan (1985), p. 7.
34. Thomas and Bilchik (1985), p. 476.

References

Academy for Contemporary Problems. 1981. *Major Issues in Juvenile Justice Information and Training: Readings in Public Policy.* Columbus, Ohio: Academy for Contemporary Problems.

American Bar Association/Institute of Judicial Administration, Juvenile Justice Standards Projects. 1980. *Standards Relating to Court Organization and Administration.* Cambridge, Mass.: Ballinger.

Arkansas Advocates for Children and Families. 1983. *Due Process Rights and Legal Procedures in Arkansas' Juvenile Courts.* Little Rock, Ark.: Arkansas Advocates for Children and Families.

Criminal Justice Statistical Analysis Center, State Planning Agency. 1984. *Legal Representation in Status and Delinquency Cases.* St. Paul: Minnesota Juvenile Court.

Feld, B.C. 1984. "Criminalizing Juvenile Justice: Rules of Procedure for the Juvenile Court." *Minnesota Law Review* 69 (2).

Feld, B.C. 1987. The Juvenile Court Meets the Principal of the Office: Legislative Changes in Juvenile Waiver Statutes. *Journal of Criminal Law and Criminology* 78 (3): 471–533.

Fine, K. 1983. *Out of Home Placement of Children in Minnesota.* St. Paul: State of Minnesota.

Florida Center for Children and Youth. February 1988. Tallahassee, Fla.: *Florida Juvenile Justice Audit.*

Grisso, T. 1980. "Juveniles' Capacities to Waive Miranda Rights: An Empirical Analysis." *California Law Review* 68 (6): 1134–66.

Institute of Judicial Administration/American Bar Association. 1980. *Juvenile Delinquency and Sanctions.* Cambridge, Mass.: Ballinger.

Ito, J.A. 1984. *Measuring the Difference for Different Types of Juvenile Courts.* Williamsburg, Va.: National Center for State Courts.

Knitzer, J., and Sobie, M. 1984. *Law Guardians in New York State: A Study of the Legal Representation of Children.* New York: New York State Bar Association.

Melton, G.M. 1986. "Should the Juvenile Court Be Abolished?" American Psychological Association Division of Child, Youth and Family Services, *Newsletter* 9 (4).

Piersma, P.; Ganousis, J.; Volenk, A.E.; Swanger, H.F.; and Connell, P. 1977. *Law and Tactics in Juvenile Cases.* Philadelphia: American Law Institute.

Ryerson, E. 1978. *The Best-Laid Plans: America's Juvenile Court Experiment.* New York: Hill and Wang.

Snyder, H.N.; Hutzler, J.L.; and Finnegan, T.A. 1985. *Delinquency in the United States: 1982.* Pittsburgh, Pa.: National Center for Juvenile Justice.

Thomas, C.W., and Bilchik, S. 1985. "Prosecuting Juveniles in Criminal Courts: A Legal and Empirical Analysis." *Journal of Criminal Law and Criminology* 76 (2).

Wadlington, W.; Whitebread, C.H.; and Davis, S.M. 1983. *Cases and Materials on Children in the Legal System.* Mineola, N.Y.: Foundation Press.

Legal Cases

Faretta v. California. 422 U.S. 806 (1974).

In re Gault. 387 U.S. 1 (1967).

Kent v. United States. 383 U.S. 541 (1966).

McKeiver v. Pennsylvania. 403 U.S. 528 (1971).

Debra Lynn Walker v. Arkansas Department of Human Resources. 20 January 1987. Appeal from Pulaski County Circuit Court, No. CIV 85-10875, Supreme Court of Arkansas.

9

The Next Twenty Years

There are always those that say, "You can't do it." There are
always those that say, "No, no." "Not now." "Go slow." "Wait
awhile." There are always those that say, "Well, we used to do
it the other way. Let's continue." Had we listened to the voices
that guard the doors of the past, we wouldn't have any America.
— Hubert H. Humphrey, 31 October 1966

Juvenile Justice Reforms: Prospects for the Future

Many child advocates, juvenile justice professionals, academics, and
public interest groups feel a deep sense of frustration about what
little progress has been made in reforming the juvenile justice system
during the past two decades. Despite historic decisions by the U.S.
Supreme Court that grant juveniles some of the same due process
and procedural safeguards accorded to adults, despite the enactment
of the landmark Juvenile Justice and Delinquency Prevention Act of
1974, despite class action lawsuits that attack the conditions under
which juveniles are confined and violations of their constitutional
rights, and despite exposés in the media, widespread abuses in the
system continue to exist.

Although no one can predict what the future will hold in juvenile
justice, there is reason for optimism. The recent history of juvenile
justice suggests that the field goes through cycles of reform and
retrenchment. The current indications are that the country is
coming out of a period of retrenchment and is in the beginning stages
of a new wave of reform.

The best evidence of this reform trend can be seen in the policy activities and developments in the states, rather than in initiatives under way at the federal level. Public concern about juvenile crime is keeping this issue on the minds of state and local elected officials. The fiscal problems confronting most states, coupled with increasing demands for services, are forcing elected public officials to reexamine state and local juvenile crime prevention and control policies more objectively and realistically than has been the case in the recent past. A recent study by the National Conference of State Legislatures indicates:

> Community-based care, alternative rehabilitation strategies, overcrowded facilities and the continuing requirements of secure institutional settings for delinquent youth form the nexus of issues that currently dominate the juvenile justice agenda of state legislatures and apparently will continue to demand attention through the 1980s.[1]

More encouraging is the fact that policymakers and professionals are increasingly looking to Massachusetts and Utah—states recognized as having model youth corrections systems—for guidance in revamping their programs.

Another factor contributing to these reform efforts is the growing public awareness and concern about the plight of our children. A Louis Harris and Associates public opinion survey revealed that "nearly 3 out of 4 Americans (74%) think problems affecting children have gotten worse since they were growing up."[2] More than half of those surveyed felt that drug abuse was the most serious threat to young people. Many others felt that "child abuse, parental neglect, divorce, sexual abuse and alcohol use" were among the most serious problems confronting children.[3] What was particularly revealing was that most of the respondents felt that "government is spending too little on programs for children" and that they would support increases in their taxes for children's programs.[4]

Governors and state lawmakers are also showing more interest in children's issues. Such issues as educational reform, infant mortality, children's physical and mental health, prenatal care, child care, child physical and sexual abuse, teenage pregnancy, substance abuse among young people, and the need to strengthen families are receiving increased attention in the states. In fact, a number of governors have declared that the needs of children and families will be a priority during their administrations.

An Action Agenda

We are in the midst of an interesting period in the history of juvenile justice. The climate in many states for initiating a rational debate on youth crime prevention and control policies appears to be somewhat favorable and is likely to become even more so in the future. The challenge we face is how to capitalize on this opportunity.

Many factors will influence the course of events in juvenile justice over the next couple of decades. None will be more important than the issues given priority by elected public officials, professionals, public interest groups, and child advocates. In my opinion, if meaningful and lasting reform is to be accomplished, the action agenda should include the following:

1. Laws should be enacted in every state to prohibit the confinement of juveniles in adult jails and police lockups. Juvenile justice and child welfare professionals, public interest groups, professional associations, and child advocates should launch aggressive campaigns in their states to help bring about such legislation. Also, where appropriate or necessary, litigation strategies should be pursued to help bring an end to such confinement of juveniles.

It has been demonstrated in a number of states (for example, Pennsylvania, Oregon, Colorado, Utah) that juvenile jailing can be reduced by 80 to 90 percent by implementing a variety of relatively low-cost programs and alternatives (for example, nationally recommended juvenile detention intake criteria, twenty-four-hour on-call crisis intervention and screening, home detention, family shelter care, and staff-operated shelter care). Also, the development of effective alternatives would minimize the number of secure detention beds needed for youth who require confinement pending their appearance in court.

2. All large training schools should be closed. These institutions are expensive to operate and difficult to manage, and they simply don't work. They have no place in an enlightened and cost-effective youth correctional system. Elected public officials and youth corrections administrators should replace these institutions with small,

high-security treatment units reserved for youth who commit serious violent crimes and for chronic offenders. The experiences in Massachusetts, Utah, Pennsylvania, and a few other states indicate that the number of juveniles who need to be confined for purposes of public protection is relatively small and that the overwhelming majority of juvenile offenders can be safely managed in a diverse network of highly structured community-based programs. Juvenile justice reforms implemented in Massachusetts and Utah have proved that this can be accomplished without sacrificing public safety and with confidence that individual rates of reoffending for those placed in community programs can be significantly reduced. In implementing such a strategy, policymakers should explore how existing youth detention and correctional resources might be more wisely reinvested. In many instances, the resources currently tied up in the financing of large training schools can be reallocated to support the operation of small (fifteen- to twenty-bed), high-security treatment units as well as community-based programs.

In a number of states (for example, Missouri, Oklahoma, Kentucky, Pennsylvania, Utah, Maryland, Massachusetts, Florida), large state training schools have been closed. These states represent interesting and diverse examples of public-sector strategies for bringing about change. Although much can be learned from the experiences in these and other jurisdictions, much can also be learned from the private sector. For example, such successful private-sector change strategies as offering cash settlements to employees, cashing out employment retirement programs, developing early retirement programs, and combinations of these approaches should be looked at very carefully. Some of these strategies are already being used in the public sector, particularly in the area of education. However, they are not being utilized to any significant extent in the youth corrections area, although they could prove to be particularly effective in states where employee unions, employment in small rural communities, and the like, are major obstacles to reform.

3. Any serious efforts to restructure state and local youth detention and correctional systems should include plans to involve the private sector in the delivery of services. It has been shown that the active involvement of the private sector can lead to the development of a diverse and innovative network of services capable of meeting a

broad range of security and individual program needs. In Massachusetts, approximately 50 percent of the entire Department of Youth Services budget is contracted out to private vendors.

4. Approximately 60 percent of the juvenile justice cases referred to the courts each year are for minor and petty crimes and for status offenses.[5] To the extent possible, the minor delinquency cases should be diverted from formal court processing, and the status offense cases should be removed from the jurisdiction of the courts altogether. This would allow the court to focus their attention and resources primarily on youth who commit Part I crimes—the crimes the public is most concerned about. Experience in many jurisdictions suggests that many of the minor delinquency and status offense cases can be dismissed without the need to take further action. In cases where a dismissal may not be appropriate, greater emphasis should be placed on requiring that offenders pay restitution to victims or perform community service.

The system of voluntary social services for status offenders needs to be both expanded and improved. Also, mediation and dispute resolution programs should be made available for these cases. Status offense cases are often rooted in family problems. Because mediation services are designed to help strengthen families by helping family members resolve disputes and conflicts, they are ideally suited for many of these cases. In instances where noncoercive measures prove to be ineffective and a determination is made that a child's health and welfare is endangered, officials should initiate action under state dependency and neglect statutes.

5. Juvenile court jurisdiction ends at age 18 in most states. However, it ends at age 17 in Georgia, Illinois, Louisiana, Massachusetts, Michigan, Missouri, South Carolina and Texas, and at age 16 in New York, Connecticut and North Carolina. In those states where juvenile court jurisdiction ends under age 18, it should be raised to end at the age of majority.

The experiences in virtually all of the states where juvenile court jurisdiction ends at 18 indicate that the overwhelming majority of those who commit serious, violent crimes and those who persist in committing serious property offenses can be managed in the juvenile justice system without compromising public safety. Treating juveniles as adults when they are 16 or 17 years old may seem appealing as a "get tough" measure. However, there is no credible evidence that such policies are effective crime control measures. Moreover, in view of the recidivism data (referred to in chapter 1) pertaining to juveniles released from Florida's prisons, there is reason to believe that they may even be counterproductive.

Raising the age of juvenile court jurisdiction will be viewed by many as a political impossibility. They will argue, therefore, that it's an issue that isn't worth spending time on. I have no illusions about how difficult it may be to make any headway on this issue. Nevertheless, I think this is an objective well worth pursuing. In those states where the age is lower than 18, large numbers of juveniles are being thrown into adult correctional and prison systems—systems that are bankrupt, violent, and devoid of any meaningful rehabilitative capacity. We are fooling ourselves if we think that the youth who inevitably return to the streets from these systems will be law-abiding and productive citizens.

6. State lawmakers should enact legislation to grant juveniles the same due process and procedural protections accorded to adults. Such legislation should also provide juveniles with an unwaivable right to counsel. This unwaivable right to counsel is needed in light of research indicating that children 15 years of age or younger who waive their right to an attorney generally do not understand the full significance and implications of their decisions.

7. Laws should be enacted to open up delinquency proceedings in the juvenile court to the public and the media. There is far less need for confidentiality to "protect" juveniles than for opening up the courts to public scrutiny and accountability.

8. The parens patriae model of the juvenile court should be laid to rest. It should be replaced by a model emphasizing that the fundamental role of the court in delinquency matters is to dispense justice. Moreover, the juvenile courts should be courts only and should get out of the business of administering detention centers, youth correctional services, and related social service programs. Since it is doubtful that most of the juvenile courts that run such programs will relinquish them voluntarily, state lawmakers should enact legislation mandating that juvenile detention facilities, youth correctional services, and other youth treatment and rehabilitation programs operated by the juvenile courts be administered by an appropriate agency within the executive branch of government.

The juvenile courts should have the capacity to monitor dispositions. They should be provided with modest, but adequate, resources to determine the results of their dispositions—whether services are being delivered and whether they are being provided in a timely fashion—and to be able to assess the relative quality of youth detention and correctional programs.

9. It is hard to imagine improving the quality of justice for children without addressing the need to upgrade the structure and quality of the juvenile court. Although there may be a variety of ways to accomplish this objective, none is more important than seeing to it that the most competent and able individuals are appointed or elected to serve on the juvenile court bench.

10. Juvenile probation programs need to be overhauled. Hundreds of millions of dollars go into the financing of juvenile probation services each year. Much of this money is being wasted, however, because probation largely consists of providing youth with minimal supervision, coupled with threats of retaliation or "consequences" if they fail to obey rules set down by the court and probation staff. This can hardly be construed as effective public protection or meaningful rehabilitation; in large part, it accounts for the widespread perception that juvenile probation is nothing more than a "slap on the wrist," not a particularly credible sanction. Furthermore, a recent study measuring the effectiveness of different levels of probation services in the Salt Lake County Juvenile Court calls into question whether the traditional concept of probation is even relevant today.[6]

11. There is a desperate need to reduce the excessive use of predispositional detention. Based on the experiences in Genessee County, Michigan, and elsewhere, it is not unreasonable to expect that the rates of detention can be cut by 50 percent or more in most communities without compromising public safety.

12. Policymakers and professionals should put an end to the "short, sharp shock"—the practice of committing youth to serve time in juvenile detention centers. Detention centers were never intended to house pre- and postdispositional populations under the same roof, and the comingling of these groups poses significant programmatic, legal, and administrative problems. On a more practical level, it's an expensive practice of dubious value. On average, it costs taxpayers more than $2,000 each time a youth is committed to a detention

center.[7] A recent study in England found that a high percentage of youth subjected to the "short, sharp shock" treatment and rigid "military-style discipline" had high rates of recidivism compared to youth sentenced to community-based alternatives.[8]

13. Policymakers, child advocates, health care experts, professional medical associations, health care planning organizations, public interest groups, and groups interested in health care cost containment must turn their attention to the unprecedented and alarming growth in the number of juveniles being propelled into private hospitals and other residential settings for inpatient psychiatric and chemical dependency treatment. Specifically:

a. Legislation should be enacted in every state to ensure that children confronted with the prospect of being confined against their will for psychiatric or chemical dependency treatment have adequate due process and procedural protections.

b. Parents should be encouraged to seek a second and truly independent medical opinion when faced with a recommendation to hospitalize their child for psychiatric or chemical dependency treatment.

c. Legislation should be enacted to require that all hospitals and private residential facilities providing psychiatric treatment for children be monitored on a regular basis.

d. Mandatory insurance laws and health care insurance programs should be reexamined and, if appropriate, modified to provide financial incentives encouraging the use of outpatient services over inpatient care. In particular, consideration should be given to requiring consumers to pay for part of the hospitalization costs for psychiatric or chemical dependency treatment as a way of discouraging the use of inpatient treatment for these disorders.

e. Outpatient psychiatric and chemical dependency services for children and families need to be greatly expanded. There is a critical shortage of intensive home-based services, day treatment, respite care, and specialized family foster care—services that would minimize the need for inpatient treatment.

14. The federal government's track record in juvenile justice since the enactment of the Juvenile Justice and Delinquency Prevention Act of 1974 has been considerably less than distinguished. The OJJDP has been riddled with politics, has been poorly managed, and has never lived up to the national leadership expectations the

Congress, the juvenile justice community, child advocates, and others had for it. Nevertheless, the Juvenile Justice and Delinquency Prevention Act and the federal juvenile justice program should be preserved and, if anything, strengthened.

Federal involvement in juvenile justice is needed to support and stimulate research activities; to initiate and carry out carefully selected demonstrations of broad national significance; to serve as a clearinghouse for information to professionals, elected public officials, professional associations, public interest groups, child advocates, and the public at large; to provide technical assistance and consultation; and to give leadership and encouragement for the adoption of enlightened juvenile crime prevention and control policies and practices.

As stated earlier, it is doubtful that any progress would have been made in removing juveniles from adult jails if it were not for the Juvenile Justice and Delinquency Prevention Act. Although it is debatable whether much of the block grant funding allocated to the states has been used by the various state juvenile justice advisory committees to comply with this initiative, the prospect of losing federal funds because of failure to meet the mandate to remove juveniles from jails and lockups has proved to be a powerful mechanism for helping to bring about change at the state and local levels. Also, the mere fact that the U.S. Congress has spoken on this issue, has declared that removing juveniles from adult jails is a national priority, and has felt that this goal was of such importance that it was specifically written into the act itself has served as a model for states to follow. For instance, some of the actors who were instrumental in the enactment of the recent jail removal legislation in California acknowledge that the legislation probably never would have passed if it weren't for the jail removal amendment to the federal act. Individuals in other states where juvenile jail removal legislation has been enacted or is under consideration have made similar observations.

Whenever the Juvenile Justice and Delinquency Prevention Act comes up for reauthorization, there is always a debate about whether the act should be reauthorized as is or modified in some way. The fear of key congressional staff members, child advocates, state juvenile justice advisory committees, and others is that if the act were "opened up" for serious debate, something awful might happen—regressive amendments might be added to the legislation or it might not reauthorized. I feel that the act should always be the subject of objective and thoughtful debate. I also believe that the act and the federal juvenile justice program needs to be restructured. The unbridled discretion the administrator of the OJJDP has to give out funds on a noncompetitive basis needs to be reigned in. New amendments should be added that will encourage state and local policymakers to improve the quality of justice for children. Also, the OJJDP should be encouraged to use fiscal and other incentives to help bring these changes about. Providing incentives for change would serve as a constructive motivator, rather than simply punishing states for failing to live up to their obligations, as is now the case. When the amendment to remove juveniles from adult jails passed, our intention was to use some of the OJJDP's discretionary funds as incentives for the states to make progress on this vital issue. Attorney General Civiletti approved a substantial increase (34 percent) in the OJJDP's fiscal year 1981–82 budget because we were able to make the case that additional resources were needed to accomplish this objective and because we wanted to use some of the discretionary funds in this way.

The persistent and widespread problem of children being abused in public and private youth detention and correctional facilities can no longer be ignored by the federal government. There must be strong and consistent federal leadership if the problem is to be eliminated or, more realistically, minimized. Accordingly, the Congress should require that states receiving federal juvenile justice funds adhere to constitutional and generally accepted professional practices and standards for the care and treatment of children. Federal officials, particularly the administrator of the OJJDP, should take a leadership role in bringing this issue to the attention of the public and in encouraging juvenile justice professionals, state and local elected public officials, public interest groups, and others to do something about it.

Also, the funds appropriated for the federal juvenile justice effort need to be increased significantly. The OJJDP has been lucky to survive the persistent attempts by the Reagan administration to kill the program. However, the fact remains that the office has been underfunded since it was created, and this has been a major impediment to accomplishing of the goals embodied in the act.

15. The federal government has been the largest investor in juvenile justice research during the past ten years. Despite the fact that the investment has been relatively meager and has not always been invested as wisely as it could have been, some of the results have been extremely valuable. However, there is a critical need to advance knowledge in this important area. It is essential that the federal government substantially increase its spending for juvenile justice research and, at the same time, take more care in defining and furthering the national juvenile justice research agenda. We need to learn much more about the interconnections between the juvenile justice, child welfare, and children's mental health systems; about promising strategies for preventing serious and chronic juvenile criminal behavior; about how best to treat youth with serious drug, alcohol, and mental health problems; about which specific intervention strategies work best with youth who exhibit various kinds of delinquent behavior; about what can be done to prevent the large influx of minority youth into the juvenile justice system; and about how best to reintegrate violent and chronic offenders back into the community.

16. Relatively few private foundations are active in juvenile justice. The few that were turned their attention elsewhere when the large federal dollars started pouring into criminal and juvenile justice in the late 1960s and early and mid-1970s. Because we are in a period when the prospects for bringing about significant and lasting change are promising, foundations should quickly and carefully explore the opportunities in juvenile justice and should consider investing in this area. In particular, foundation support is needed for activities that the government won't fund (for example, system monitoring and advocacy by private groups, litigation, studies and reports on selected and controversial issues, and public education). Also, foundation support can be instrumental in launching important demonstrations and in facilitating systemic changes.

A Broader Social Agenda

In the long run, it is sheer folly to think that we will be able to tackle the juvenile crime problem effectively without addressing some of the country's broader domestic issues. The development of effective juvenile crime prevention and control strategies will ultimately hinge upon our ability to educate our children, to provide them with adequate housing and health care, to reduce youth unemployment (particularly for minorities), to prevent and respond effectively to child abuse and neglect, to provide adequate child care, to strengthen families, to prevent drug and alcohol abuse, and to eradicate poverty. Poverty is a particularly devastating problem, and it engulfs a large number of children. Despite the often-heard rhetoric that "children are our greatest natural resource," children are the largest disadvantaged group in the United States today. They account for approximately 40 percent of all the people living in poverty.[9]

> One of the most alarming consequences of the growth of poverty in this country is the impact it has on the health of pregnant women and children. In particular, fewer women have been receiving prenatal care and fewer children have been receiving preventive health care since 1982 than had been the case previously. As a result, the incidence of infant mortality, premature birth, and low birth weight is up in many states, and immunization against childhood disease has declined dramatically. These children are more likely to grow into chronically ill adults and inadequately educated or trained workers.[10]

It is also apparent that there is a large and growing underclass in our society, particularly in urban areas. This population is poorly educated, unskilled, and unemployed. This problem has been allowed to mushroom, despite

> data that show that individuals who experience unemployment are, in fact, more likely to have higher rates of crime. One recent investigation of young, unemployed black males explicitly concludes that "a fundamental influence on criminal behavior is the role of economic factors, such as labor market status. Respondents who were in school or employed were much less likely to engage in crime."[11]

However, as Duster points out in his thoughtful analysis of this issue, the problem of youth unemployment, particularly for black youth, will not be corrected with "simple solutions." The changes in the labor force require that efforts be made to equip youth with the skills needed to successfully enter into and compete in today's labor market as well as to move up the career ladder.[12]

Discussion

Recent attempts to reform our nation's juvenile justice system have had limited success. The results fell far short of expectations because the reform efforts largely occurred during a period when the states were in a retrenchment mode. We are now in a period in which the climate for reform is becoming more favorable. In fact, the indications are that policymakers and opinion leaders in more than half the states are in the process of rethinking their juvenile crime control policies and, in some instances, restructuring their youth detention and corrections systems.

In this chapter and, indeed, throughout this book, I have identified what I believe to be some of the most critical issues confronting our juvenile justice system, particularly those that will help to ensure justice for children. Although I believe that progress on these issues will have a significant and lasting impact on our ability to respond to the juvenile crime problem in a rational and effective way, we cannot expect to make any serious headway on the prevention front until we address the broader domestic public policy issues that confront our society.

Notes

1. National Conference of State Legislatures (1988), p. 1.
2. Harris (1986), p. 4.
3. Ibid.
4. Ibid., p. 2.
5. Snyder, Hutzler, and Finnegan (1985), p. 7.
6. U.S. Department of Justice (1987).
7. Schwartz et al (1987).
8. *London Times* (1986).
9. Economic Policy Council of UNA-USA (1985), p. 3.
10. Ibid., p. 54
11. Duster (1987), p. 302.
12. Ibid., p. 312

References

Duster, T. 1987. "Crime, Youth Unemployment, and the Black Urban Underclass." *Crime and Delinquency* 33(2): 300–316.

Economic Policy Council of UNA-USA, Family Policy Panel. 1985. *Work and Family in the United States: A Policy Initiative.* New York: United Nations Association.

Harris, L. 1986. *Children's Needs and Public Responsibilities: A Survey of Public Attitudes About the Problems and Prospects of American Children.* National Survey for Group W (Westinghouse Broadcasting Company). New York: Louis Harris and Associates.

$186,710 For Your Thoughts. London Times. March 1986.

National Conference of State Legislatures, February 1, 1988. Youth Corrections Survey. "Current Juvenile Justice Issues Facing State Legislatures." Denver, Colo.

Snyder, H.N.; Hutzler, J.L.; and Finnegan, T.A., 1985. *Delinquency in the United States: 1982.* Pittsburgh, Pa.: National Center for Juvenile Justice.

Schwartz, I.M., Fishman, G., Hatfield, R.R., Krisberg, B.A., and Eisikovits, Z. 1985. "Juvenile Detention: The Hidden Closets Revisted." *Justice Quarterly* 4(2): 219–235.

U.S. Department of Justice, Office of Juvenile Justice and Delinquency Prevention, and National Council on Crime and Delinquency. 1987. *The Impact of Juvenile Court Intervention.* San Francisco: National Council on Crime and Delinquency.

Index

About the Author

I RA M. SCHWARTZ is a professor of social work and director of the Center for the Study of Youth Policy at the University of Michigan in Ann Arbor. He formerly was a senior fellow at the Hubert H. Humphrey Institute of Public Affairs at the University of Minnesota and from 1979 to 1981 served as administrator of the Office of Juvenile Justice and Delinquency Prevention in the U.S. Department of Justice.

Mr. Schwartz has also served as executive director of various state and national criminal and juvenile justice reform organizations and as a consultant, both nationally and internationally. He has authored and co-authored numerous articles on juvenile justice, child welfare, and children's mental health.

Mr. Schwartz received an M.S.W. degree from the University of Washington.

DATE DUE

APR. 27 2000			
AUG. 04 2000			
NOV. 27 2001			
GAYLORD			PRINTED IN U.S.A.